HERBERT KARL KALBFLEISCH

THE HISTORY OF THE PIONEER GERMAN LANGUAGE PRESS OF ONTARIO, 1835-1918

The History of the Pioneer German Language Press of Ontario, 1835-1918

by Herbert Karl Kalbfleisch

1968

University of Toronto Press

First published in Canada 1968 by University of Toronto Press
Reprinted 2017
ISBN 978-0-8020-1579-2 (paper)

Dedicated

to the

German Pioneers

of

Ontario

TABLE OF CONTENTS

LIST OF ILLUSTRATIONS

ZUM GELEIT

Folke Dahls Grundsatz, Zeitungswissenschaft als eine internationale Forschungsaufgabe zu sehen und zu betreiben, hat sich auf dem Arbeitsfeld des schwedischen Zeitungshistorikers — der sich entfaltenden europäischen Presse des siebzehnten Jahrhunderts — als besonders fruchtbar erwiesen. Aber er gilt nicht nur dort. Im Blick auf anderes erkennt man eigenes; Originales stellt sich im Vergleich heraus. Ein Urteil über ein Ganzes wiederum läßt sich nur fällen, wenn man die Einzelheiten geprüft hat. Nationale Presseforschung darf den Blick über die Grenzen nicht vergessen; international betriebene benötigt eingegrenzte Vorarbeiten, muß, so meint Dahl, auf „nationalen Grundsteinen" aufbauen. Die „Deutsche Presseforschung" bei der Staatsbibliothek Bremen konzentriert ihre Arbeit, wie ihr Name sagt, auf die deutsche — das meint: deutschsprachige — Presse. Damit will sie im Sinne Folke Dahls einen Beitrag zur internationalen Presseforschung leisten. Dies zeigt sich auch in der von ihr betreuten Buchreihe. In ihr erschienen Icko Ibens Übersicht über die Presse der Benelux-Staaten und Skandinaviens („The Germanic Press of Europe", 1965) — durch die das eigentliche Arbeitsgebiet der „Deutschen Presseforschung" sogar verlassen wurde — und 1961 die erste Auflage von Karl J. R. Arndts und May E. Olsons Bibliographie der deutsch-amerikanischen Zeitungen und Zeitschriften — durch die ein umfassender Überblick über diese historisch wie sprachlich noch kaum erforschten Zeugnisse deutsch-amerikanischer Geschichte ermöglicht wurde. Die deutschsprachige Presse Kanadas hat keine so lange und bedeutende Entwicklung durchlaufen wie die der Vereinigten Staaten. Gleichwohl können die von deutschen Einwanderern und ihren Nachkommen in Kanada herausgegebenen Blätter als sozial-, kultur- und sprachgeschichtlich ergiebige Quellen angesehen werden. Sie harren noch weitgehend ihrer Erschließung. Der vorliegende Band wird wesentlich dazu beitragen, Charakter und Wert dieser Quellen kennenzulernen, indem durch einen berufenen Kenner die deutschsprachige Presse Ontarios als historisch abgeschlossenes Phänomen vorgestellt wird. Ich danke Herrn Professor Kalbfleisch von der University of Western Ontario in London (Kanada) dafür, daß er die Aufnahme seiner Darstellung in unsere Buchreihe ermöglicht hat. Herrn Professor Arndt von der Clark University in Worcester/Massachusetts sei auch an dieser Stelle Dank für seine Anregung gesagt, das Werk seines kanadischen Kollegen zu veröffentlichen. H. K. Kalbfleischs Bericht über die deutschen Zeitungen Ost-Kanadas ist in englischer Sprache abgefaßt und wird in der Alten wie der Neuen Welt vertrieben. Möge er hier wie dort Interesse wecken und Freunde finden!

Elger Blühm

PREFACE

The flourishing period of the pioneer German-language press of the province of Ontario, Canada, falls into the second half of the nineteenth century. Already by 1900 its forward course had been severely checked by the process of fusion and assimilation of the German minority into the English-dominated pattern of Ontario.

Although the abrupt ending of the first phase of German newspaper publication in the province in 1918 came in consequence of an arbitrary act on the part of the then government of Canada, it must be assumed that, without strong reinforcement of the German-speaking community of Ontario, the continuation of German-language newspapers, even without the advent of the first World War, would have presented serious problems.

The German newspapers of the earlier period — approximately thirty in number — which flourished for longer or shorter periods between 1835 and 1918 — wielded little influence and attracted almost no attention outside of the Ontario German settlements. The German population was never numerically large enough to exert any major impact on social and political thinking. The German newspapers were essentially local weekly papers in every sense of the word. They printed and interpreted what was transpiring in the outside world and domestically to their clientèle, without making any serious attempt to shape the course of events, except at times on a purely local level.

The large influx of German immigrants into Ontario, as well as into other areas of Canada, after the second World War has prompted a modest revival of the German newspaper press. It may be assumed that this revival will again take on the proportions of a flourishing period, to be followed by a gradual decline as the forces of integration wean away the readers into the dominant cultural and linguistic patterns of their respective communities.

The German immigrant of today is inclined to adapt himself much more quickly to the pattern of his surroundings than was his predecessor of the nineteenth century. The urge to settle in closed communities is noticeably absent. There is no "clearing-house" in our day, such as Waterloo County represented to the German newcomer of the nineteenth century. Through this lack of rallying points the urge to perpetuate the language and the culture of the homeland has been considerably weakened. Nevertheless a history of the second, and geographically larger, phase of German journalism will some day have to be written.

Although the secular German newspapers provided the major bulk of early German journalism in Ontario, there were also German religious periodicals published by the various German church groups. These existed coevally with the secular newspapers, but catered particularly to the religious denominations which sponsored them.

Newspaper files have furnished the basis for most of the facts and conclusions presented in this account. During a period of several years the author has read the files of the extant German-language newspapers of Ontario. These files were also able to provide a considerable amount of information about those newspapers which were not preserved.

The author wishes to express his gratitude to all those who helped in the production of this study. He is particularly indebted to the officers of the Waterloo Historical Society for permission to use the excellent collection of German newspaper files in the Society's museum, to Peter Fisher, late secretary of the Waterloo Historical Society for his generous suggestions, to Miss Dorothy Shoemaker, chief librarian of the Kitchener Public Library, to Mr. Ernst Ritz of New Hamburg for the loan of his files of the *Canadisches Volksblatt*, but above all to his wife, whose pertinacity in seeing this study brought to a conclusion may in large part be ascribed to her Pennsylvania-German background, which provided the link between the early German settlers in Ontario and that of the author's family, which migrated from Hesse in the 1840's.

Herbert K. Kalbfleisch.

CHAPTER I
INTRODUCTION

The history of the pioneer German newspaper press in the Province of Ontario, Canada, covers a period of less than one hundred years. Its initial as well as its final chapter was written in the same town, namely Kitchener (formerly Berlin), Ontario.

Ontario was, however, not the first province in Canada to entertain a migration of German people. Hanoverian subjects of George II of England were recruited for the settlement of Nova Scotia, when the English decided to set up an outpost there as a check to French expansion to the south, at the end of the fifth and the beginning of the sixth decade of the eighteenth century. Between 1750 and 1752 approximately two thousand Germans came into the Halifax and Lunenburg areas. Three decades later their number had increased to approximately three thousand.

By sheer coincidence a German printer appeared in Halifax toward the end of the 1750's in the person of Anthon Henrich (Anthony Henry) and to him falls the honor of having done the first German printing in Canada.

Anthon Henrich was born in Alsace in 1734 of German parents. He had been apprenticed to a printer but had left his employ and migrated to the New World where he became a fifer in a British regiment, from which he was discharged at Perth Amboy, New Jersey, in 1758. From there he made his way to Nova Scotia where he became a partner in the printing-office of John Bushell, the printer and publisher of the *Halifax Gazette* (founded 1752) and the official government printer. The *Gazette* is reputed to have been the first newspaper published in Canada[1].

Bushell died in 1761, whereupon Henrich took over the printing establishment, although barely twenty-seven years of age. He also continued as the official government printer, from which source he derived a yearly income of between sixty and one hundred pounds.

In 1766 the government revoked his patent because of Henrich's critical attitude toward official policy, and for some time a competitor received the government's printing account, but several years later Henrich was restored to favor and his contract was renewed.

During 1769—1770 he issued the *Nova-Scotia Chronicle and Weekly Advertiser,* and from 1770 on the *Nova-Scotia Gazette and the Weekly Chronicle*, the latter of which vied in make-up and content with the better American journals of its day.

In 1769 Henrich issued an annual calendar in English for the first time. It bore the title *The Nova-Scotia Calender, or an almanac for the year of the Christian Aera, 1769.* He continued issuing an annual calendar from that time on until his demise.

But Henrich also cherished the dream of publishing a German newspaper in Nova Scotia [2]. He was very proud of his mother tongue and felt called to restore it to its rightful place in his adopted province, although he realized that many of the younger generation did not share his enthusiasm. He proposed to issue a German weekly, to appear every Friday with the title *Die Welt, und die Neuschottlaendische Correspondenz* (The World and the Nova Scotian Newsletter), which was to contain the most important events transpiring in the world, and for which he would employ English newspapers as his news sources, supplemented by the most interesting items from the local scene. A German almanac was also projected. This latter plan became a reality when Henrich issued *Der Hochdeutsche Neu-Schottländische Calender, auf das Jahr, nach der heilbringenden Geburt unsers HErrn JEsu Christi, 1788* (The High German Nova Scotian Calendar for the year 1788 after the blessed birth of our Lord Jesus Christ). This almanac followed more or less the pattern of the many publications of this order appearing in the colonial and Revolutionary period of American history. Its chief claim to historical renown stems from the fact that it gave an account of the arrival of the first German settlers in Nova Scotia.

Henrich's German newspaper, of which no copies are preserved, was conducted by a German journeyman printer, Henry Steiner, who had come to America as a Hessian mercenary in the Revolutionary War[3]. He arrived in Halifax in 1782, where he was mustered out and immediately thereafter began working for Henrich. The German types used in the printing of the German newspaper were procured from Justus Fox, in Germantown, Pennsylvania. The German weekly was of relatively short duration, appearing only between 1787 and 1789. Its demise came when Steiner went to Philadelphia in 1789. Two factors seem to have conspired against its success: there were too few subscribers, and there was considerable competition from German newspapers and periodicals from Pennsylvania.

Anthon Henrich died in December 1800, sixty-six years of age. He had been named King's Printer in 1788, a position which assured him of a permanent yearly income from the public treasury.

There is no evidence of any further attempt to publish a German newspaper in the Canadian maritime provinces after Henrich's somewhat ephemeral venture came to an end.

Henrich's German newspaper in Nova Scotia was designed for readers who had migrated to Canada before the main French bastion in Quebec and its western hinterland had come under British control. In fact, almost forty years had elapsed since the first wave of German migration had come to Nova Scotia and appearance of Henrich's *Die Welt*. We must marvel that the German minority still retained its language and can only conclude that their state of local isolation was such that they were not assimilated into the English pattern.

With the British conquest of Canada the land was thrown open for immigrants. But there was no rapid influx from any quarter into this vast undeveloped wilderness.

The revolt of the American colonies and the assertion of their independence also followed so closely on the heels of the British takeover in Canada that a feeling of apprehension and uncertainty was evident in would-be immigrants to the north of the new and restless United States. There was no organized German immigration into the new land. German troops had served in British garrisons in Canada during the early years of occupation and during the Revolutionary War. As many as 2500 are believed to have remained after their discharge. They were to be found as artisans in the small towns or as farmers living in the villages in much the same manner as in the homeland, or domiciled on their holdings, or as farm workers on the seignories in the townships along the St. Lawrence in Quebec, in the Annapolis Valley in Nova Scotia, on the lower St. John in New Brunswick, and in parts of eastern Ontario. They did not in any way represent solid pockets of settlement and were gradually absorbed into the local communities.

The province of Upper Canada, as Ontario was then called, became the beneficiary of a considerable migration that began to flow in consequence of old loyalties in the struggle for independence from the motherland on the part of the American colonies. These loyalist settlers, still known in our day as United Empire Loyalists, counted among their number many people of German antecedents, including Hessian troops who had served in the British armies during the war and who, after being mustered out in the colonies at the war's end, decided to make their permanent home in the new world.

But the bulk of the German migration from the former American colonies after the Revolutionary War consisted of Germans who had settled in New York State, where loyalty to the mother country remained somewhat more fervent than elsewhere in the thirteen colonies during the struggle for independence. Many of these were Palatines from Duchess County, and from settlements on the Mohawk and Schoharie Rivers. Their loyalty to the British cause made a further stay in the new republic a dubious venture and consequently more than one thousand of them migrated to eastern Ontario in the Morrisburg-Williamsburg area in Dundas and Stormont Counties, to the Bay of Quinté west of Kingston, and to the Niagara Peninsula. A small number even made its way to the Maritime provinces of New Brunswick and Nova Scotia.

Those who came to Ontario still spoke the German tongue on their arrival. However, surrounded as they were by English and Scottish colonists, and lacking German teachers and preachers, they gradually lost command of the German language and assimilated into the local pattern. Their numbers would in any case have precluded the establishment of a German newspaper press on a successful economic basis.

Further settlements by Germans from the United States before 1800 were made in the Counties of Haldimand, Welland, and Lincoln in the Niagara Peninsula, as well as in Markham Township of York County. Their descendants inhabit these areas until the present day, and some of them have not completely given up their devotion to the language of their forefathers, even though what they may retain does not measure up to a good standard.

It was, however, not until Waterloo and adjacent counties in the more south-westerly part of the province were settled that a solid enough group of people speaking and reading the German language was assembled in one area to make a German press a feasible venture. Even then it did not follow immediately after the Mennonite migration into Waterloo and surrounding areas, which began in 1800. The Mennonites did not consider a secular press necessary to their happiness, as they depended for their edification mainly on religious papers and books. However, as immigrants began to arrive from Germany who were not Mennonites, first in small numbers around 1820, and then in larger groups after 1830, the necessity of a secular newspaper began to manifest itself.

Waterloo County, then, in the heart of south-western Ontario, became the German stronghold in this province. It still has to this day a preponderance of German names, and some pioneer German customs linger on. The German language, however, except for remnants surviving in the local dialect chiefly in the rural areas, has almost disappeared. The descendants of the German pioneers no longer read the files of the German newspapers of the nineteenth and early years of the twentieth century to discover what their ancestors did, thought, and read.

There are, of course, some among the many immigrants from the German lands who arrived after the second World War who are taking an interest in the earlier German migrations. Theirs is but a historical interest. They cannot see with the eyes of those early settlers what this country offered in joys, sorrows, and disappointments as well as in satisfactions to those who came in earlier times from the German-speaking areas.

What has happened in this regard in Waterloo County is also true elsewhere in the former German-speaking settlements. In the counties of Huron, Perth, Grey, Bruce, Welland, in the cities of Hamilton and Toronto, and on the banks of the Ottawa, where a settlement of Germans, particularly in Renfrew County, was made after 1850: in all these areas where German was once read and spoken it exists among the pioneer group only as a memory. Time and circumstance have militated against the perpetuation of the German language among the pioneer settlers everywhere in Ontario. There is nothing left but a rich store-house of information about the German settlements contained in the German newspaper files which chronicled their week-by-week story.

The early German settlers who came to Canada were mainly farmers and artisans. They were not illiterate, however. Their desire for belletristic material was, in part, satisfied by the German newspapers. Books were difficult to obtain and considered expensive in a country where land and wood were plentiful, but where money was in short supply.

European, and particularly German, news was given much space in the early Ontario German newspapers. For some years after his arrival the German, in common with other European immigrants, still found his spirit across the water, while his physical self sojourned in the new land. Time altered this and gradually a new loyalty came into being. The German newspapers assisted in this process by acquainting the newcomer with the geographical, historical and political background of his adopted land. At the same time they softened the blow of the sudden displacement. It must be noted that an easy tolerance on the part of the English-speaking majority in Ontario helped materially to lighten the labor of fusion and assimilation of the German minority.

There is little hope that any interest, beyond that of a purely academic nature, may be aroused in the record preserved by the pioneer German newspapers in Ontario. Some sentiment is still evident toward the culture from which they sprang, but the chief pride of the older-established German communities in Ontario is that they made a worthwhile contribution to the country of their adoption, and have earned the right to fit into it as good and loyal citizens. The incidence of two World Wars, in which Germany was twice the enemy, has dampened the ardor for a revival of German language newspapers in the areas in which they once flourished.

The German newspapers naturally represented only a small segment of the total amount of journalistic activity in Ontario while they existed. They did, however, represent the only foreign language newspaper press in Ontario at that time. Since most of them were printed and published in the smaller communities they must be categorized as village or small-town weeklies. Their spread from one town to another was often the work of journeymen, who wished to go into business for themselves in a promising location as yet unsupplied with a German newspaper. The success or failure of such a venture was, consequently, largely governed by the concentration of an easily accessible German-language group.

CHAPTER II

THE BEGINNINGS, 1835—1850

The flow of new settlers into Upper Canada, as Ontario was called after 1791, continued apace after the first wave of immigration in the 1780's. Although the original German participation in this flow was, as has been noted, not very considerable, it nevertheless marked the beginning of a migration which was to bring a fairly substantial group of German people to the new province.

Of particular importance is the first far-inland settlement in Upper Canada, Waterloo County, in which people of German antecedents, both from Pennsylvania and later from Europe played a major rôle.

The immigrants from Pennsylvania formed the vanguard of this settlement. An attempt in the year 1795 to bring a relatively large and compact group of Mennonites to Ontario did not find a sympathetic response from the then governor of Upper Canada, John Graves Simcoe, and was abandoned. Scattered Mennonite settlers, however, did migrate into the general area of south-western Ontario, paving the way for a systematic migration after 1800.

It was this Mennonite migration which provided the impetus for the later influx of settlers directly from Germany. It provided a bridgehead for German-speaking newcomers and remained as such during the major portion of the nineteenth century.

It was in the little hamlet of Berlin, Waterloo Township, that the first German weekly newspaper in Upper Canada appeared. The date was August 27, 1835, and the weekly was the *Canada Museum und Allgemeine Zeitung*. Its editor and publisher was Heinrich Wilhelm (later Henry William) Peterson, who was born in Quakenbrück, in the Duchy of Oldenburg, Germany, May 27, 1793.

Heinrich Wilhelm Peterson was two years of age when his parents migrated to America, settling temporarily in Baltimore, Maryland. In 1796 they left Baltimore and moved to Blue Ball, only to leave this locality again in 1799 to go to the County of Kleets, where his father began to preach and teach Sunday school. Another move took the family to Harrisburg, Pennsylvania, where it arrived in March, 1803. In 1810 the father was ordained as a preacher in the Lutheran Church, and served various parishes in Somerset County, Pennsylvania, for the next nine years.

In February 1819 the Peterson family left Pennsylvania, as the father had accepted a call to become the minister to Lutheran congregations in Markham and Vaughan Townships, north of Toronto, in the Province of Upper Canada. In 1824, as the result of a dispute in his congregation,

Peterson resigned from the Vaughan Church. He continued his work in other congregations of the district until old age forced his retirement. He died in 1848, at the age of 91 years.

Henry William Peterson, who became the editor and publisher of the first German newspaper in Upper Canada, had not accompanied his parents when they moved to Canada. He had remained in Pennsylvania and entered newspaper work there. At Carlisle, Pennsylvania, he published a German newspaper from 1814 to 1817.

In 1823 or 1824 he visited Canada for the first time, returning shortly afterwards to Wilmington, Delaware, where he married Hannah Ann Hendrickson on June 9, 1825. She died in 1830 at the age of 23 years. Peterson at the time operated a printing shop at Dover, Delaware. For a short period he published the *Legislative Reporter* and later the *Christian Magazine*. Both ventures failed for lack of support. Peterson is credited with the distinction of having been the first American journalist who proposed Andrew Jackson for the presidency of the United States.

In 1831 Peterson married again, this time the widow of Walter Douglas, a daugther of James Clayton and sister of John M. Clayton, Secretary of State of the United States under President Zachary Taylor, and co-author of the Clayton-Bulwer Treaty between the United States and Great Britain. After this marriage the Petersons moved to Canada permanently, going first to the father's home in Markham where, on December 13, 1831, a son was born to the couple. In 1832 Henry William Peterson first visited Waterloo Township. Although not an ordained preacher, he began to minister to the German people of the Lutheran faith. He was a deeply religious man but not given to bigotry, proof of which he provided by visiting and attending church with Benjamin Eby, the Bishop of the Mennonite Society of Waterloo, whose piety and goodness he extolled.

Mrs. Peterson followed her husband to Berlin in 1833. The family lived under the most primitive conditions in the tiny settlement, but there is nothing in the record of pessimism or complaint on the part of Mrs. Peterson, who had exchanged a life of luxury and comfort for one of deprivation and inconvenience in a backwoods settlement. Her husband's printing ventures had never been lucrative, and there was no indication that Berlin would be the place where his fortunes might change, as it was a tiny place, lacking even a post office. However, by 1835 Peterson was in the printing business again. He did not have the capital necessary to open a printing establishment, but friends, to the number of over a hundred and forty, came to his aid, and made it possible for him to secure the needed equipment. Of this number, fifty-one became shareholders in the company by virtue of the size of their subscription, a share of twenty dollars entitling the subscriber to one vote[1]. The list of the shareholders' names, and the promised or paid subscriptions were published in the first issue of the *Museum*.

The resolution embodying the desires of the benefactors of the new venture was indeed sincere in tone, even if, at times, rather quaint in expression. In translation, it reads as follows:

A Proposal
for the establishing of a printing office in
Waterloo Township

Since it is the universal and sincere desire of the Germans of Upper Canada that a German newspaper and also German books might be published in this country, and since the desired opportunity presents itself at this time to set up a good printing office here in Waterloo; and indeed such a one in which every kind of necessary English printing can be carried out; but since the printer is financially unable to purchase the same, we, the undersigned, desire to purchase the printing office for him, that is to say in the following manner:

Each one of us who pays twenty dollars is to have one share in the undertaking; whoever pays thirty dollars is to have a share and a half, and whoever pays forty dollars is to have two shares in it, etc. We as shareholders consequently own the printing office, and provide our money for it for a period of five years without interest, in order that the venture may have a sound beginning, and may continue to flourish under our patronage. If however the printer, Peterson, wishes to purchase the printing office after the aforesaid five years have elapsed, he shall have the permission to purchase the same from us, that is, if he repays us the money which we now advance him.

He must annually (if we so desire), beginning with the first year, pay back at least two dollars per year. And should he not repay the monies advanced to him after the expiration of the abovementioned five years, he must then pay us the legal rate of interest on our money.

We promise to pay our shares for which we have subscribed between now and the first of May, 1835.

Given under our hand, on the fourth day of March, 1835.

Ninety-five additional friends and well-wishers of the new venture did not contribute sufficiently large sums to become shareholders, but their contributions materially assisted in putting the business on a sound foundation.

Some of the shareholders seem to have been carried beyond their actual financial resources by their enthusiasm, and seem not to have paid their subscriptions on the date they were due, May 1, 1835, and, in some cases, they were probably never paid at all. Peterson never referred to the tardy ones by name, in order not to give offence, but there were reminders that he could use the money which had been pledged as early as January, 1836.

Peterson's financial support came largely from the Mennonite immigrants from Pennsylvania. Their interest in the publishing of a German newspaper and the printing of books in the German language is readily understood. They were a minority conscious of their background, and anxious to preserve the traditional values which meant so much to them. One of these values was the German language which, although somewhat diluted by English influence during their stay in Pennsylvania, remained a holy tongue, since it was the language of their divine services.

The new printer, publisher and editor had the confidence of these immigrants. His pious, gentle attitude toward all struck a responsive chord in their hearts and inspired their generosity toward him.

Peterson's printing press was transported by oxen from Pennsylvania.

Schubert's Lied,

An die Würtembergischen Truppen die nach dem Cap der Guten Hoffnung gesandt wurden.

Auf, auf! ihr Brüder! und seyd stark,
Der Abschieds-Tag ist da;
Schwer liegt er auf der Seele, schwer,
Wir sollen über Land und Meer,
In's heiße Afrika, :,:

2.

Ein dichter Kreis von Liebe steht,
Ihr Brüder, um uns her!
Uns knüpft so manches feste Band
An unser deutsches Vaterland:
Drum fällt der Abschied schwer, :,:

3.

Es bieten graue Eltern noch
Zum Leztenmal die Hand,
Dem guten Bruder, Schwester, Freund,
Und alles klagt und alles weint:
Ist blaß von uns gewandt, :,:

4.

Und wie ein Geist, schlingt um den Hals,
Das Liebchen sich herum;
Willst mich verlassen, liebes Herz,
Auf ewig!—und der bange Schmerz
Machts arme Liebchen stumm, :,:

5.

Ist hart! d'rum wirb'le du Tambour,
Den General Marsch darein:
Der Abschied macht uns sonst zu weich,
Wir weinten kleinen Kindern gleich:
Es muß geschieden seyn! :,:

6.

Lebt wohl ihr Freunde! sehn wir uns
Vielleicht zum Leztenmal,
So denkt nicht, daß die kurze Zeit,
Freundschaft ist für die Ewigkeit:
Denn Gott ist überall, :,:

7.

An Deutschland's Gränzen füllen wir
Mit Erde unsre Hand,
Und küßen sie—dies sey der Dank,
Für deine Pfleg, Speise, und Trank,
Geliebtes Vaterland! :,:

8.

Wann dann die Meereswoge sich
An unserm Schiffe bricht,
Dann segeln wir gelassen fort,
Ein Gott ist hie, ein Gott ist dort,
Und der verläßt uns nicht! :,:

9.

Und ha! wenn sich der Tafelberg
Aus blauen Dünsten hebt,
Dann heben wir empor die Hand,
Und jauchzen laut: "Ihr Brüder, Land!"
Daß unser Schiff erbebt, :,:

10.

Wann dann Soldat und Offizier
Gesund an's Ufer springt;
Dann jauchzen wir "Ihr Brüder, ha!
Nun sind wir ja in Afrika!"
Und alles springt und singt, :,:

11.

Dann leben wir in fernem Land,
Als Deutsche brav und gut;
Und sagen soll man weit und breit,
Die Deutschen sind ja brave Leut,
Sie haben Geist und Muth, :,:

12.

Und trinken auf den Hoffnung Tag
Wir feinen Götterwein;
Dann denken wir von Sehnsucht weich,
Ihr fernen Freunde, auch an euch,
Und Thränen fallen d'rein, :,:

Berlin, (Ober Canada) Gedruckt von Heinrich Eby....1835.

In August, 1835, it was set up in Berlin and the first printing was done on it. The accompanying poem, Schubert's *(sic)* Lied, provides a good example of the clear, clean copy the *Museum* press could produce. Heinrich Eby, the printer of the poem and Peterson's first apprentice, was destined to play a considerable rôle in the development of the Ontario German press.

It is quite possible that Eby printed the *Lied* for a local resident who, for some reason or other, desired a printed copy of this famous work by Christian Daniel Schubart, 1739—1791. Schubart was a minor writer of the eighteenth century Storm and Stress movement in Germany, whose satiric fulminations against Duke Karl Eugen of Württemberg resulted in a ten-year detention for the author in the Württemberg fortress of Hohenasperg. The intervention of Frederick the Great of Prussia eventually secured his release.

This poem usually appears under the litle of *Das Kaplied.* It is the song of the conscripts sold by Duke Karl Eugen to the Dutch East India Company for service at the Cape of Good Hope during the latter part of the eighteenth century.

The *Museum* was a weekly with a subscription price of two dollars per year. One dollar was payable at the time of subscription and another dollar at the end of six months. From time to time the day of publication fluctuated between Thursday, Tuesday und Saturday, and occasionally a week, or several weeks, were marked by the non-appearance of the *Museum* because of the editor's ill-health. The first volume, for example, covers the period from August 27, 1835, to October 20, 1836. A year for Peterson meant fifty-two issues, even though a period of more than twelve calendar months was necessary to produce them.

Peterson directed an energetic appeal to all literate Germans in Upper Canada to subscribe to the *Museum.* He appointed a certain Samuel Horner to solicit subscriptions for the paper in the Waterloo area, and named agents for it, among whom was his own father in Markham, in other German communities throughout the province.

The *Museum* never grew beyond four pages in size. In the beginning the pages were 10³/₄ inches wide and 17 inches high. The second volume saw a slight increase in size to 13¹/₂ inches wide and 19¹/₂ inches high. Four wide columns were used throughout; the quality of the paper was uniformly good and the print clear. There was considerable variety in the size of type used, but no deliberate attempt seems to have been made to emphasize important news by using larger type.

The masthead of the *Museum* bore, in addition to its title, the coat-of-arms of Great Britain inserted between the words *Canada* and *Museum.* A poetic motto of four lines, evidently the work of the publisher and editor, appeared directly underneath the caption [2].

Editorially the *Museum* reserved the right to criticize the government of the province; it pledged itself to assist in preserving peace and quiet among the diverse elements in Upper Canada, and to warn against any disturbers of the peace; it promised to bring local and foreign news, to feature the useful arts and sciences and to indicate the activities of local governing bodies.

Although primarily a German newspaper, the *Museum* made considerable concessions to those among its readers who, at times, wished to have some reading material in the English language. The editor realized that there were many German subscribers who could not read English, and usually begged their indulgence on such occasions. English and German advertisements often stood side by side, and frequently the articles advertised were featured in both languages.

The *Museum* hat its inception in stirring times in the Canadas. Economic conditions were bad; there was widespread dissatisfaction with the provincial legislatures in both Upper and Lower Canada and with many local governing bodies as well. Rebellion was in the air. People everywhere sensed the tension and began to take sides for or against the prevailing authority. The *Museum* attempted to be politically impartial and neutral. It largely favored the government in power, it seems, because the editor was a peace-loving man who abhorred the use of force, even in a righteous cause. He made no secret of his adherence to the established authority, and urged his readers at all times not to take part in any rebellious enterprises. When the rebellion finally broke out in 1837, Peterson addressed earnest admonitions to his German readers not to become involved. In two extras to number fifty-one of volume two, dated December 12, 1837, he provided the chief events of the rebellion and, in the second extra, he pleaded once more with all to remain calm and not to risk death or loss of property. Peterson was proud to note that the Germans on the whole remained peaceful, although he knew that many of them were opposed to the government.

With the beginning of the third volume of the *Museum* on December 23, 1837, Peterson was joined by Christian Enslin, a local bookbinder, as associate editor. This partnership was dissolved on November 22, 1838, after lasting approximately one year. Enslin had come to Berlin in 1833, and he died there in 1856. After severing his connection with the *Museum* in 1838 he seems to have bided his time with the intention of returning to journalism as soon as the opportunity presented itself. This opportunity came relatively quickly and we find him as editor of the *Deutscher Canadier*, the successor to the *Museum* at the beginning of 1841.

In June, 1839, the *Museum* suddenly was faced by a competitor in the neighboring village of Waterloo. Peterson gave a polite and generous welcome to the newcomer, although no one knew better than he that there were not enough subscribers and advertisers in the immediate German community to support two German newspapers at that time.

His editorial words of June 15, 1839, are not without humor, although tinged with a note of apprehension:

Last Saturday evening a *Morning Star* (Morgen-Stern) appeared in our neighborhood. But all punning aside! We want to explain this natural phenomenon or seeming contradiction clearly at this point. This *Morning Star* is the first number of a German newspaper issued by Messrs. Burkholder and Company in the town of Waterloo. It is being printed to a large extent with new type. The reason for the first number appearing in the evening, may be ascribed to the arrangement of the multifarious details, which always and everywhere accompany such a laborious business.

The *Morning Star* does not clearly indicate any political allegiance, nor whether it is for or against our present government, nor whether it is Whig, Conservative, Tory or Reformer, and this is perhaps not very important. What is clear, however, is that it looks forward to the support of a liberal public, and such support — namely a liberal one — we sincerely wish for the new publisher and editors, as well as a prosperous future in their difficult and expensive undertaking. The Germans in Canada now have the choice of two newspapers in their mother tongue. We hope that no one will continue to complain of a lack of adequate coverage of government affairs; we hope everyone will be satisfied now.

We believe that Messrs. Burkholder and Company will make an honest effort to produce a fine and useful newspaper. They are people of acumen, and their praiseworthy effort to inform and be of use to their fellow men deserves a generous response from the German public. May they soon enjoy a large list of prompt subscribers, as well as many good friends and supporters.

The villages of Waterloo and Berlin were only in their infancy at this time. Berlin had approximately twenty-five houses in 1835. A large body of support for the German newspapers consequently had to come from the rural community. Peterson catered particularly to the Mennonite group, which formed a very considerable proportion of the German-speaking population in Waterloo County. His influence made itself felt particularly through the deeply religious and quietistic attitude of the *Museum* and, in addition, he was well and favorably known through personal association with many members of the Mennonite communion.

By 1840 the *Museum* appeared even more irregularly than before. The reason given was lack of help in the print shop. Peterson had always been a public-spirited man. His interest in public matters consumed a major portion of his energies and did not permit him to spend the required amount of time on the *Museum*. His sustained agitation procured a post office for Berlin, as well as the appointment of a justice of the peace. This latter office was given him in 1838, making him one of the first justices of the peace in the Western District. In 1840 he was appointed Registrar of the District of Wellington, with headquarters at Guelph. It became evident to him that he could not publish a newspaper and, at the same time, adequately discharge the duties of the other offices which devolved on him. He, therefore, sold the German part of his printing establishment to Heinrich Eby, the son of Bishop Benjamin Eby of the Mennonite community, who had served as an apprentice to him for four years and was well qualified as a printer. With number 26 of volume 5, Peterson took leave from his readers [3]. He recommended the new German newspaper, *Der Deutsche Canadier*, which was to be published by Heinrich Eby and Christian Enslin, to all former subscribers of the *Museum*.

In addition to the *Canada Museum*, Peterson's press had also printed a German song book in 1836. This song book was the first German book to be printed in British North America. German almanacs were also published by Peterson for the years 1838, 1839, 1840 and 1841.

To Henry William Peterson, an enterprising and courageous immigrant, must go the credit for inaugurating the German newspaper press in Upper Canada. A German newspaper could exist only if it received good support from the community, which in pioneer times was largely rural in character. It is true that villages were dotted here and there over the Waterloo landscape as elsewhere, but they were small, and some of their inhabitants were frequently farmers in the tradition of the German "Dorf". The *Museum* recommended itself specifically as a newspaper for the German farmer and the German artisan. Peterson did his best to cater to the desires of his clientèle. He attempted to steer a neutral course in the political sphere, and maintained a fervently religious tone throughout. The *Museum* carried something for everyone. Poetry by known and anonymous authors was featured in almost every number. Local poets, among whom the editor also must be counted, were given space. Here one often finds high enthusiasm wedded to restricted talent; nevertheless, such activity assisted in keeping up local interest in German literature, as well as in the German school, the newspaper, the sermon and German customs generally. Religious verse finds frequent inclusion but the larger bulk is secular in tone. Representative of the better known poets are Graf Friedrich von Stolberg, Theodor Körner, M. G. Saphir, Heinrich Heine, Nikolaus Lenau, Julius Mosen and others. The work of local versifiers and anonymous poets was of much greater volume than that of the more outstanding writers. Much of the poetry was drawn from German exchanges in the United States, which source also yielded the major portion of the literary prose material, as well as the foreign news.

The continued story made a modest debut in the *Museum*. This was an item that was heavily featured by the successors to the *Museum*. However, Washington Irving's *Astoria* and Heinrich Stilling's *Florentin von Fahlendorn* ran on an instalment basis during the earlier period of the *Museum*. Very short stories and articles, usually gay, but sometimes lurid or tragic, were provided as weekly fare for the inquisitive. However, Peterson, as a religious man, leaned toward a presentation of the more restrained prose material.

Political, social and economic events in all countries were always covered. This material came from exchanges and was often no longer fresh when it reached *Museum* readers. Local gossip was almost completely lacking. Here the *Museum* differed radically from later German weeklies which had correspondents scattered far and wide over the German-speaking area who reported news of a more intimate character.

Peterson was a man with a mission. He wished to make his beloved Germans, as he called them, aware of their importance in Canada[4]. While he upheld the German language, he sought in other departments, to integrate the Germans into the Canadian scene. He wished to make them politically conscious by presenting in his news reports, as well as in his editorial columns, the latest events in the political field in Canada and to acquaint them with the machinery of government under which their adopted land operated. He ran articles explaining the constitution of Great Britain to his readers, and in general made an honest effort to enlighten his fellow-countrymen of German antecedents with the advantages, political and otherwise, of the new land. Although he urged his readers to remain aloof from the subversive events of 1837, and himself remained a supporter of the existing government in the Canadas, one can feel that at heart Peterson was a liberal. That he advocated non-intervention on the part of the Germans in the Rebellion of 1837 doubtless stemmed from his desire not to permit them, as a minority non-English group, to acquire the reputation of not obeying constituted authority. In spite of his admonitions, a few Germans became involved in rebellious proceedings. One of them, Gottlieb Eckhardt of the Markham district, was arrested and imprisoned at Toronto. Also a shareholder in the *Museum*, Anton (Anthony) van Egmond, of Huron County, although of Dutch antecedents, suffered a similar fate, and later died in prison in Toronto.

Anton Jakob Wilhelm Gispert, Lamoral, Baron van Egmond, was, without doubt, the most illustrious benefactor of the *Museum*. He was a descendant of a distinguished noble family of the Netherlands, a sixteenth century ancestor, Count van Egmond (German, von Egmont) having been executed at the behest of Philip II of Spain in Brussels on June 5th, 1568, on a charge of treasonable activities against the Spanish rulers of the Netherlands. Anton, Colonel Anthony van Egmond, as he appears in Canadian historical records, was born in 1771. When he was eighteen, the French Revolution broke out. Holland was later overrun, and Anthony was conscripted into the French army. He served in several campaigns in this army, including the ill-fated march on Moscow, until Napoleon's defeat, and was badly wounded in the battle of Waterloo. In 1819 he migrated to Pennsylvania and eight years later came to Canada. He took up land near the present town of Seaforth in Huron County, and is credited with having harvested the first wheat in the so-called Huron Tract.

Van Egmond was a very publicly minded man and in addition an enlightened thinker in politics. He soon clashed with the policies of the Canada Land Company which had been organized to develop a huge tract of land bordering on Lake Huron. He branded these policies as parasitical, and viewed the officials of the Company as incompetent and as seeking to please the ruling clique in the Canadas, the "Family Compact". His opposition to the Company crystallized into open criticism of the government, whose inept handling of public affairs prompted him eventually to espouse the cause of William Lyon Mackenzie. This open participation in the abortive rebellion in Upper Canada unfortunately cost him his life. Van Egmond, as a former professional soldier, was entrusted with the military aspects of Mackenzie's revolt. He soon realized that a small, inadequately armed group could not cope with an attack by a numerically superior, well-disciplined militia. His participation in the clash at Montgomery's Tavern on Yonge Street on December 7th, 1837, was the final public act of a man who had played a significant role in the pioneer annals of Western Ontario.

Peterson's *Museum* had been very proud of the fact that Van Egmond had supported its founding. It made very favorable mention of his part in the settling of Huron County in an article of September 15, 1836. It was visibly embarrassed that he had become embroiled in the rebellion but nevertheless paid a fulsome tribute to him in its issue of January 27, 1838. Van Egmond had died on the second last day of December, 1837, probably from pneumonia induced by exhaustion. He was buried on January 14th, 1838, at Ross, in the Township of McKillop, in the Huron Tract.

Despite these actions of one of its shareholders, the *Museum* repeatedly urged the Germans in Ontario to engage in legitimate political activity, and suggested that they elect one of their number to the legislative assembly. Peterson felt that there were capable men among them who could make a constructive contribution to Canadian political life.

The *Museum* made a modest concession to the local German dialect by occasionally employing some English words which had found their way into the local vocabulary. A random selection shows *Trosties* (trustees), *machte eine Spietsch*, *Stohr* (store), *Kamp-Mieting*, *Settlementer*, and *Häfner-Schap* (shop). In the main, however, a fairly good standard of language was maintained. There are some eccentricities in spelling at times, but some of these deviations may safely be attributed to hasty proof-reading.

A good volume of advertising was carried by the *Museum*. Generally pages three and four were largely given over to advertising material, but the first page at times also carried a column or two in addition to the news articles, literary prose and miscellaneous items which normally appeared there. Various business houses, professional men, manufacturers, money-lenders, etc., publicized their wares. Public notices, market prices, birth, death, as well as many notices requesting information regarding missing persons, round out the advertising columns.

There is no way of discovering the number of subscribers that the *Museum* had from time to time. Peterson gave the impression that his venture was successful from that angle, but he failed to reveal definite figures. It may safely be assumed that his subscription list was never large, containing at most perhaps several hundred names. A flourishing subscription list would surely have indicated a continuation of the *Museum* instead of its rather precipitate termination with number 26 of volume 5 on December 18, 1840.

Peterson's newspaper did much to publicize the Waterloo area among the German-speaking people in Canada and the United States. The steady growth of the German population of Berlin and its surroundings after 1835 must, in part, be attributed to the splendid advertising qualities of the *Museum*. That the English-speaking people of Canada were also aware of the existence of the *Museum* is indicated by a reference to it by a contemporary traveler who noted that "a paper in the German language is published at Berlin in the Gore district, for the use of the German settlers"[5].

In 1843 Peterson moved to Guelph, where he lived until his death on June 12, 1859.

It is virtually impossible to obtain more than intelligent estimates on the number of German immigrants living in the province of Ontario in the 1830's. The usual assumption is that there were approximately 20,000 in three main areas, eastern Ontario, the Niagara peninsula, and the Waterloo County area. A steady flow of newcomers from the German lands probably doubled this figure by 1848. Of these, 15,000 lived in eastern Ontario and 25,000 in the western part of the province. The census of 1871 gives us an inkling how rapid the influx of new German settlers must have been, as the total number of German settlers is given as 158,608. These were distributed as follows: 116,189 in south-western Ontario, 41,743 in eastern Ontario, and 676 in New Ontario.

If in Peterson's day he had to rely primarily on the Germans in south-western Ontario for support — and this is a relatively safe assumption — he would naturally not be anxious to welcome competition for the meagre number of eligible subscribers and advertisers, but this is precisely what *Der Morgenstern* in Waterloo provided for him when it entered the field in 1839.

Peterson had accordingly several reasons for transferring his newspaper into other hands, in addition to having a competitor. Ill-health plagued him at times; there was a dearth of German type-setters — a common complaint; the appointment to a government position — indeed several positions — which all impinged on his time: first as a justice of the peace, and then as registrar of the District of Wellington with headquarters in the neighboring town of Guelph, approximately eighteen miles from Berlin. This latter appointment removed him almost completely from the German community, Guelph being primarily an English-speaking town with English-speaking surroundings.

Der Deutsche Canadier, the lineal descendant of the *Canada Museum und Allgemeine Zeitung* still had its Waterloo competitor *Der Morgenstern* in the field when it made its appearance.

Der Morgenstern was published for the first time on June 8, 1839, on the outskirts of Waterloo Village by Benjamin Burkholder. It was a weekly of four pages, 20½ inches tall and 13 inches wide, with four wide columns per page. Its subscription price was $ 1.50 at the beginning of the year, $ 2.00 after six months, $ 2.25 if in arrears, and $ 2.50 if received by mail. There was a slight upward revision in these rates at the end of the first year of publication.

Der Morgenstern resembled the *Canada Museum* in many respects, although its tone, in general, was lighter and somewhat more secular. Even its motto, *Recht und Gerechtigkeit ohne Ansehen der Person* (Right and justice without respect of persons), sounded a great deal like the motto of the last year of the *Museum, Wahrheit und Gerechtigkeit* (Truth and justice). Pages three and four were generally reserved for advertising matter, although this depended, as with the *Museum*, on the quantity of advertising material available week by week.

Poetry, prose, political news — local, Canadian and foreign — the useful arts, scientific articles, and interesting items of all sorts filled the pages of the *Morgenstern*. The bulk of this material came, as with the

Museum, from exchanges. A typical, but only partial, list reveals the following sources: *Ohio Staats-Zeitung, Buffalo Weltbürger, Allgemeine Zeitung, Toronto Colonist, Ceres, Lancaster (Pa.) Volksfreund, Anzeiger des Westens, Harrisburg Vaterlands-Wächter, Lecha Patriot, Alte und Neue Welt, Canada Museum, Hamilton Express, Niagara Chronicle, New York Herald, New-Yorker Staatszeitung.*

The *Morgenstern* laid little emphasis on intimate local news and local gossip, although it reported in detail the proceedings of local governing bodies and other official local news. Otherwise its columns, exclusive of advertising, dealt chiefly with events removed from the immediate scene. The Act of Union of the Canadas was covered in detail in six issues of October and November, 1840. Simultaneously the terms of the new Militia Act were announced. The issue of responsible government in Canada was given detailed discussion. By publishing this material the *Morgenstern* made accessible to those German readers who were unable to read English a picture of the Canadian political panorama, and also provided some insight into Canadian political organization for German immigrants from Europe who, at this time, were beginning to arrive in larger numbers.

European news, with particular emphasis on Germany, was always in abundance. Major political events in the United States were faithfully chronicled. Other parts of the world likewise received mention if their news was considered to be of sufficient importance.

The poetry section carried mainly anonymous verse, or poems of minor German poets. The serious, the humorous, and the sentimental were represented in this section. The quantity of poetry, as well as of fictional prose, indicates a sustained interest by the readers in literary material. Entertainment, rather than literary excellence, was the criterion applicable to the *Morgenstern's* literary offerings. There was little serial prose. Most of the prose stories were concluded in one issue, although there were a few exceptions.

The *Morgenstern* did not eschew sensational items. Stories of murders and executions are frequent, and the reader is not spared any of the lurid and harrowing details often associated with such events.

The usual advertising matter is heavily supplemented with notices of the wonders that can be wrought by liniments and nostrums of every sort. This material constituted a sure income for the publisher and was, no doubt, necessary for financial survival at a time when national advertising had not yet been developed.

It was evident that Burkholder had overestimated the capacity of the German population in Ontario to absorb newspapers when he began *Der Morgenstern*. Yet he cordially greeted *Der Deutsche Canadier* when it made its appearance in January 1841. It soon became evident, however, that the German community could, or would, not support two German newspapers, and even if the desire to support a second newspaper had existed, the subscription price would surely have been a serious deterrent. This was certainly the case, as we see from Burkholder's own admission, in a land where ready cash was relatively rare. That

Der Morgenstern deserved support is clear. Its editor, in spite of obstacles, made a determined effort to produce a weekly which presented something for everyone, and he presented it in an attractive manner. That he did not succeed in establishing himself lay not in his own effort, but rather in a situation over which he had no control: he had arrived too soon. *Der Morgenstern* was compelled to suspend publication; its last issue is dated September 16, 1841. Beginning with the number appearing on August 26, 1841, the "star" which had headed the editorial column as the symbol of *Der Morgenstern* began to wane. The editor quite philosophically gave warning that his newspaper would have to cease publication after a few more numbers. The reasons given were a heavy debt on his printing establishment, and the tardiness of both subscribers and advertisers in discharging their financial obligations to the publisher. As the "star" slowly became smaller during the last three weeks of publication, Burkholder pleaded with his debtors to pay their outstanding accounts. With the money he hoped to pay for his press and equipment and, although he did not expect to publish a German newspaper again, he planned to remain in the printing business — at least on a part-time basis. He proposed to establish an English and German school in Waterloo Village, and inserted an advertisement in the final number of the *Morgenstern* giving his rates and regulations. He recommended *Der Deutsche Canadier* to the readers of *Der Morgenstern*, a generous gesture toward a more successful rival.

Benjamin Burkholder later taught schools in various parts of Waterloo County, including the village of Berlin, until about the year 1873. In 1876 he was placed on the list of pensioned school teachers, on which he remained until his death in 1898. He, unlike Peterson, had been born in America — in Lancaster County, Pennsylvania — in the year 1814. In 1818 he had come to Canada with his parents where he later learned the printing trade. He was equally fluent in the German and English languages. To this fact must be attributed his later success as a school teacher.

The publishers of German newspapers in Ontario had to contend with several problems which were generally peculiar to a foreign-language press. One of these was a chronic shortage of German printers and type-setters. The other was an even more critical one: most of the news items and articles had to be translated into German from English exchanges. Both Peterson and Burkholder complained about this laborious exercise. Naturally the more specialized material provided the greatest difficulties, but this was precisely the material which both newspapers felt constrained to provide for their readers in the troubled days of political and social upheaval in the Canadas which witnessed their short existences.

The first German newspaper that did not fall into the ephemeral category was *Der Deutsche Canadier und Neuigkeitsbote*, later *Der Deutsche Canadier*, of Berlin. Its first publisher and owner, Heinrich Eby, was the son of the venerable bishop of the Mennonite community of Waterloo, Benjamin Eby, and therefore of a family whose reputation was well established in the area. Its first editor, Christian Enslin, was a Berlin bookbinder, who had for some time been Peterson's partner on, as well as associate editor of, the *Canada Museum*. Enslin, too, was well and favorably known in the district. He had migrated from Württemberg in 1833 to Canada and set up a business in Berlin. In addition to binding books, he also sold books, patent medicines, eye-glasses and other articles of a specialized nature. He became subsequently a Commissioner of the Court of the Queen's Bench, a notary public, the clerk of the Surrogate Court in 1853, and treasurer of Waterloo County in 1854. He died in Berlin on March 29, 1856.

For more than twenty-four years, from January, 1841, to January, 1865, the *Canadier* was a regular visitor to many German homes in Ontario. During this period, however, it had a succession of owners, publishers and editors.

Christian Enslin remained as editor of the *Canadier* for the first nine years. He was succeeded in that position by Johann Jakob Ernst, who had been a school teacher prior to the taking over of the editorial position. After an editorship lasting from January, 1850, to the end of June, 1853, Ernst made way for F. B. J. Schwarz who, in turn, was replaced by Edward Lindemann in October, 1853. It seems that Schwarz had become involved in difficulties of some sort or other, but the references are vague and inconclusive. Lindemann, who had been an assistant editor of the New York *Criminalzeitung*, was a political refugee from Germany. Born an October 22, 1810, at Mauersburg in the Vogtland, he had studied theology and philology and was serving as the principal of a secondary school in Zwickau, Saxony, when the revolution of 1848 broke out. As an avowed crusader in the cause of freedom, he took part in the abortive uprisings in Dresden and in Baden-Palatinate. He fled to Switzerland and from there to the United States, where he arrived before the end of 1849. For approximately four years he labored as a journalist there before coming to Canada in 1853 as editor of the *Deutscher Canadier* in Berlin. After two and a half years he resigned his position with the *Canadier* to take over editorial duties with the *Hamburger Beobachter*, in New Hamburg, Ontario. He remained, however, only a few months with the *Beobachter*. Lindemann's subsequent journalistic career saw him holding positions in Chicago, on the *Cincinnati Volksfreund*, the *Anzeiger des Westens* in St. Louis, the *New Orleanser Deutsche Zeitung*, and since 1868 on various German papers in St. Louis, where his wife was one of the mainstays of the St. Louis theatre.

Lindemann was also a man of literary aspirations. One of his own short stories appeared in the columns of the *Canadier* in December, 1853, and another serial story, adapted from a Spanish source, in 1854. He raised the quality of the *Canadier* appreciably and improved its literary tone. An English contemporary, Kirby's *Niagara Mail*, gave the *Canadier* a considerable accolade for its excellence in an article of May 3, 1854, which the *Canadier* naturally reproduced in its issue of May 11. Lindemann provided articles on German-American literature and also informed his readers on the latest importations from Europe in modern as well as German literature of the older periods, for which he acted as agent and importer.

At the end of 1851 the *Canadier* changed ownership. Heinrich Eby sold the newspaper to his brother, Peter Eby. The new owner claimed a subscription list of close to one thousand in the first issue of volume twelve on January 2, 1852. There is, however, no way in which this figure may be verified. A large subscription list was often claimed, then as well as later, to attract merchants and others to advertise their wares in the German newspapers. In April of 1856, Friedrich Keller became the editor of the *Canadier*. His tenure of this position was very short since he resigned as early as June of the selfsame year. For several weeks the *Canadier* was without an official editor. In July 1856 Peter Eby sold the *Canadier* to his brother, Elias Eby. The latter leased the newspaper to Patrick Clerihew, who became its printer and publisher. Clerihew promised to continue the *Canadier* as a supporter of the Reform party, and appointed Dr. H. Th. Legler as the responsible editor of the paper, with Friedrich Rittinger as foreman of the job and printing department. In 1857 Patrick Clerihew disappeared from the *Canadier* and Elias Eby, whose name formerly appeared as owner, again became its printer and publisher. In May, 1857, Dougall McDougall purchased the newspaper from Elias Eby. Dr. Legler continued as editor.

On June 23, 1858, Dr. Legler resigned as editor of the *Canadier* and shortly thereafter left Canada for Buffalo, New York. Born in Dresden Germany, in 1819, he had studied medicine, but having become entangled in the revolutionary uprising of 1848, he was forced to flee his homeland. He settled first at Troy, New York, and after a short stay there migrated to Ontario, where he opened a medical practice in Berlin. In addition to his practice he served as a newspaper editor there and in New Hamburg, and was also a member of the town council of Berlin for several years. Upon the outbreak of the Civil War in the United States he became a medical officer with the Union Army, and acted in this capacity for the duration of the struggle. At the close of hostilities he lived for some years at Evansville, Indiana, moving in 1876 to Oakland, California, where he died on April 14, 1908, at the age of eighty-nine years.

Upon Dr. Legler's retirement as editor of the *Canadier*, Dougall McDougall took over the editorial duties. In the following year the *Berliner Journal*, a new German newspaper, made its appearance in Berlin, and almost immediately a bitter feud developed between these two rivals. The younger paper, however, won out, and on January 19, 1865, the *Canadier* ceased publication. The *Journal* on January 26, 1865, dedicated a derisively humorous article to the demise of its bitter opponent:

Der deutsche Canadier

With a feeling of profound sympathy we must report that the *Deutscher Canadier* breathed the last breath of its eventful life last Thursday (January 19, 1865). It reached the age of twenty-four years, and would probably have become older, if it had not become so excited over the appearance of the *Journal* five years ago, in consequence of which it undermined its own health. The *Canadier* foretold a wretched existence for the new weekly and its speedy demise, and was so sure of its ground, that it had a gravestone ready for it on the date of its (the *Journal's)* second issue. When, however, the prophecy seemed not to go into fulfillment, the *Canadier* became so angry that it developed an incurable disease, which soon turned into galloping "subscriber consumption". This sickness became worse and worse, until finally the patient was almost completely consumed, and finally gave up the ghost on the abovementioned day. The editor is holding out hope to the public that the deceased will be quickly resurrected, but we fear that our beloved friend has been permanently removed from our midst. Whoever knew the friendly relations of the *Canadier* to the *Journal* will be able to imagine our profound sorrow at the prematurely departed, and will not withhold us his profound sympathy. We have preserved the epitaph which the deceased prepared for the *Journal* five years ago, and dedicate it here at the conclusion of our obituary to its revered memory:

"We are fine and for him it is better so."

An attempt was made to revive the *Canadier* in Waterloo Village under William Moyer as the *Deutscher Canadier Und Allgemeiner Anzeiger* in November 1867, but the venture lasted less than two years, and even then its tenuous existence was marred by violent disagreement between owner and editor. The final number of this attempted revival appeared during the first week of October 1869. Previously under the editorship of Wilhelm Raich, a *Deutscher Canadier* had begun to appear in September 1869, in opposition to Moyer's *Canadier* with which Raich had earlier been associated. Within a number of months financial difficulties necessitated Raich's precipitate disappearance from the community, an event which elicited a derisive *In Memoriam* poem from the *Berliner Journal* on January 20, 1870:

Wilhelm Raich, the newspaperman, the general factotum, bookseller, forwarder of money, ship's agent, deluder of people, picture framer, tread-cart rider, dealer of blows, etc., disappeared in the early morning hours one day last week. His tricked creditors are scratching their heads, and those who paid promptly in advance, who sent in their dollars, are cheated and swindled, for the press is in an idle state, and the vulgar little newspaper, as indigestible as its editor's blows, has gone to sleep and is dead, for the printer has fled the country. Everyone perceives from this that deception soon finds its reward. Therefore let each one be honest, good, and cut the coat according to the cloth. Those who ride high in vanity and pride will stumble and fall into the ditch. That is what happened to this shirker of duty. "For him it is fine and for us it is better so."

In appearance, particularly in its earliest period the *Canadier* resembled its immediate predecessor, the *Canada Museum*, to a marked extent. It was a weekly of four pages with four wide columns per page and measured 20 inches high and 14 inches wide. Its masthead included a motto which changed from time to time, a not uncommon occurrence in German newspapers of this period: *Gott und mein Recht* (God and my right), 1841; *Gleichheit allein ist die unumstößliche Grundlage des Rechts* (Equality alone is the firm foundation of Justice), 1855. The subscription price was $ 2.00 per year and $ 3.00 if received by mail.

By 1843 the *Canadier* had grown slightly. It was now 16 inches wide and 22 inches high, but with the same number of pages and columns. In 1844 it reverted to its initial size. By 1848 it was back to the 1843 dimensions, and the four columns per page had increased to five. In 1852 the subscription price was reduced to $ 1.50 in advance, and $ 2.00 if in arrears three months. There were now also six columns per page instead of five. During the editorship of Edward Lindemann the size of the paper was increased to $19^1/_2$ inches wide and $25^1/_2$ inches high, with seven columns per page on its four pages. The revived *Canadier* of 1867 still had only four pages. Its pages, which were 27 inches tall, and $20^1/_4$ inches wide, had eight columns per page. The subscription rates had not changed since 1852.

The flourishing period of the *Canadier* coincided with a rapid increase in the German population of Waterloo and surrounding counties. The twenty-five houses that Peterson mentioned in the *Museum* in 1835 as constituting the village of Berlin must have grown to many more by 1850. Smith in his volume on *Canada West* of 1851 says of Berlin: "This is a considerable village, containing about seven hundred and fifty inhabitants, who are principally German or of German descent . . . A newspaper, the *German Canadian*, is published in the Village "[6].

In the fatherland, the failure of the potato crop and poor grain crops in the middle years of the 1840's, and the turmoil and dissatisfaction with conditions leading up to the abortive revolution of 1848, induced many Germans to leave and seek new homes in America. Canada received only a small sprinkling of the new immigrants, but those who came settled to a large extent in the towns and villages, since they had been mainly artisans, and not farmers, in Europe. The German newspapers catered to these newcomers who, although they had fled from a system which they abhorred, desired detailed reports of the political and social events that were transpiring in the lands of their origin. They also demanded reading material of a literary nature to which the German newspapers responded after 1850, and which became visible in the increasing amount of poetry and prose, the latter often in serial form, which began to fill the pages of the *Canadier* and its rivals. The *Canadier*, like the *Museum*, carried relatively little intimate local news. It was, particularly during the first decade of its existence, largely a political journal with some literary content, and contained a fairly large bulk of miscellaneous material which comprehended many and varied subjects.

In Canadian politics the *Canadier* was very partisan. It sponsored the cause of the Reform Party with much fervor, and defended the Reformers against the accusation of rebelliousness which was sometimes hurled against them. The Reformers were represented as virtuous and honest, the Tories were at their best dishonest and at their worst, crooked. The Germans were urged to support the party of reform against the entrenched Tory oligarchy that had been ruling Canada.

The *Canadier* gave great prominence to news dealing with the revolutions in the various European countries in 1848 and brought out a small extra on March 31, 1848, giving details of the most important events reported up to that date. The material for this extra was taken from an undated extra of the *Hamilton Journal* from reports brought from Europe by the steamship Caledonia. In succinct style it provided the following:

Extra Blatt
des
Deutschen Canadiers.

Berlin, Freitag Morgen den 31sten März 1848.

Ankunft der
Caledonia.

Republick etablirt in Frankreich — Der König und die Königin in England—Trubel in Spanien und Deutschland—Ausbrüche in England und Schottland.

(Aus einem Extra des Hamilton Journal.)

Die bey dem Dampfschiff Caledonia gebrachten Neuigkeiten sind von der äußersten Wichtigkeit. Die Revolution hat sich über ganz Frankreich ausgebreitet. Alle Departemente nehmen Theil daran. Die Republik ist bestätiget und ist anerkannt worden von den Gesandten der Ver. Staaten, England, Belgien und der Schweiz.

Louis Philip und seine Königin hatten die größten Schwierigkeiten durchzukommen. Sie mußten von Bauerey zu Bauerey wandern und waren endlich so glücklich auf einem offenen Boot aus Frankreich zu entkommen, und nach England überzusehen. Die Königliche Familie und Minister sind ebenfalls in England. Die Pairs Kammer ist ausgeräumt und der Adel abgeschafft worden.

Die National Versammlung soll am 20st. April zusammen kommen, um eine bleibende Regierung zu formiren. Die Assembly soll aus 900 Mitgliedern bestehen. Das Wahlrecht soll allgemein seyn.

Die Arbeiter in Paris verursachten einigen Trubel. Die Finanzen sind in einem sehr schlechten Zustande und die Funds ausserordentlich gefallen.

Prinz Jolnville und der Herzog D'Aumale haben Jeder ein Dampfschiff zu ihrer Verfügung erhalten. Sie können wandern wohin sie wollen.

In **Bayern** ist das Volk ebenfalls aufgestanden und hat mit der Spitze des Bayonets eine Constitution verlangt. Fürst Metternich in Oesterreich hat abgedankt.

Die Russen (?) sind für eine Revolution reif und ganz Deutschland bricht aus.

In **Spanien** ist die Orleans Parthey über Haufen geworfen worden—neue Ausbrüche haben statt gefunden in Folge der Revolution in Frankreich.

In **England** fanden ebenfalls Tumulte statt, und zwar in London, Manchester, Edinburg und Glasgow.

In **Ireland** hat jedoch noch kein Ausbruch statt gefunden.

Die **Marktpreise** sind ein wenig am steigen, in Folge dieser Unruhen.

The dispatches brought by the steamship Caledonia are of the utmost importance. The revolution has spread over all of France. All departments are involved. The republic is confirmed and has been recognized by the ambassadors of the United States, England, Belgium and Switzerland.

Louis Philip and his queen were subjected to the greatest difficulties. They had to wander from farm to farm and were finally by fortunate chance permitted to escape from France in an open boat and to reach England. The royal family and the members of the ministry are likewise in England. The Upper House in the French Parliament has been abolished and the nobility as a social class has been done away with.

The National Assembly is to meet on April 20 in order to set up a permanent form of government. The Assembly is to consist of 900 members. Universal suffrage is to prevail.

The workers in Paris caused some trouble. The finances of the country are in bad shape and stocks and bonds have suffered a remarkable drop.

Prince Joinville and the Duke d'Aumale have both had a steamship placed at their disposal. They are allowed to go wherever they wish.

In Bavaria a people's uprising has likewise taken place, and has demanded a constitution at the point of the bayonet. Prince Metternich in Austria has resigned.

The Russians (?) are ripe for revolution and all of Germany is on the verge of revolt.

In Spain the Orleans Party has been thrown out; new uprisings have taken place there in consequence of the revolution in France.

In England demonstrations have likewise taken place, especially in London, Manchester, Edinburg *(sic)* and Glasgow.

In Ireland everything has remained quiet.

Market prices are rising somewhat as a result of these outbreaks of violence.

The fact that *Der Deutsche Canadier* issued the above extra was an indication with what interest the local population followed events in western Europe. The names of Metternich and others mentioned in the dispatches must have been common knowledge to its readers, some of whom had been more than casually involved in the struggle in the Canadas which led to more enlightened democratic processes in the land of their adoption.

During the fateful year of 1848 particularly, as well as in subsequent years, the *Canadier* abounded in European news. Kossuth's visit to the United States in the early 1850's was covered in detail. When the Germans of Albany, New York, fêted him and handed him a memorial blasting tyranny and extolling Kossuth's fight against it, the *Canadier* responded with its own words of adulation of the Hungarian hero and, in addition, printed verbatim the contents of the memorial. When Kossuth left America, he sent a farewell message to the Germans in America on June 25, 1852, from New York, to which the *Canadier* devoted over eight full columns.

The critical comments of German-Americans returning from visits to the fatherland find copious coverage. The reactionary atmosphere in general, the subservience to authority and the prevailing lack of freedom would make life there intolerable to the freedom-loving German-Americans.

Preoccupation with foreign events, however, did not mean that the *Canadier* neglected Canadian political happenings. Considerable emphasis was laid on the functioning of Canadian political and public institutions, which was, in part, calculated to raise the Germans who had migrated to Canada out of their lethargy toward public affairs which had characterized the behavior of many of them in the fatherland.

The attempt to arouse the Germans from their political slumber seems to have met with some success. On the occasion of Lord Elgin's signing of the Rebellion Losses Bill in 1849, the German inhabitants of Waterloo, Wilmot, Wellesley and West Woolwich Townships sent him a memorandum of approval of his action. Also the Mennonites and Tunkers in the western part of the Wellington District were likewise moved to send an address lauding Elgin's stand. Elgin graciously acknowledged these gestures. Election time found many letters in the *Canadier* discussing the issues and the merits, or otherwise, of the respective candidates. Yet in purely local affairs, such as the election of German school trustees in predominantly German areas, a lack of solidarity manifested itself among the German immigrants.

To acquaint its readers with new developments in public instruction, the *Canadier* printed the School Act for Upper Canada, which established public schools and provided for their maintenance, in its issue of January 19, 1844. The *Canadier* campaigned vigorously for German instruction in the local elementary schools as early as 1851, and was frequently incensed at the slow progress made in providing such instruction. All of the German newspapers kept this theme before their public. It was a matter of life and death to them that German language study be perpetuated, at least as far as a good reading knowledge was concerned. The fundamental problem, however, as far as the school authorities were concerned, was to find time for a German hour on the crowded timetable of the schools, and also to procure teachers who were sufficiently bilingual.

Another institution which fostered interest in the German language and received consequently enthusiastic support from the *Canadier* was the *Turnverein*. The first *Turnverein* in Berlin was founded on July 7, 1855, with Edward Lindemann, the editor of the *Canadier*, as one of the chief organizers. Toronto, Hamilton and Preston already had active *Turnvereine* by this time. The first annual ball of the Berlin *Turnverein* was held on December 31, 1858, an event which preceded a period of very energetic theatrical activity on the part of the *Turners*. This activity was warmly supported by the *Canadier*, because it fostered an interest in German language and culture generally, although the theatrical offerings of the *Turners* can hardly be said to have represented the zenith of literary and dramatic excellence. There are bright spots occasionally in the offerings which lead one to assume that facilities and personnel were factors inhibiting more ambitious attempts, rather than a lack of appreciation of what was good, or a deficiency in taste. Typical dramatic presentations by the Berlin *Turnverein* as revealed by the *Canadier* for 1859 were as follows: *Der Nachtwächter, Lustspiel in einem Akt* by Theodor Körner and *Der Wechsel, Vortrag in jüdischer Mundart* by Hrn. Bl. (February 18, 1859); *Richard's Wanderleben, Lustspiel in vier Aufzügen*, by G. Kettel (March 8, 1859); *Englisch oder die*

Liebeserklärung eines Engländers, Lustspiel in 2 Akten, by C. A. Görner (April 21, 1859). In an annual *Turner* celebration held in Preston in September, 1859, the *Canadier* records the following dramatic offerings: *Die Belagerung von Saragossa oder Pächter Feldkümmels Hochzeit, Lustspiel in vier Akten,* by August von Kotzebue; *Die Pute, Eine Scene aus dem Leben Heinrichs des Vierten,* and *Die Drillinge* (September 23, 1859). The centenary of Schiller's birth was celebrated by the *Turners* on November 10, 1859. Members recited several of his best known ballads, as well as excerpts from his dramas. Included in this recital was the *Festlied der Deutschen in Amerika zur Feier von Schillers hundertjährigem Geburtstage* by the well-known German poet, Ferdinand Freiligrath. Schiller was one of the most popular German poets among the pioneers in America [7]. He appealed not only to the German community, but in translation was also acclaimed in English-speaking circles. His *Wilhelm Tell* was performed in translation in Toronto as early as 1854. Somewhat later *Louise Miller* and *The Robbers* were presented there, as well as a play entitled *Mary, Queen of Scots,* apparently based on Schiller's *Maria Stuart.* Other adaptations and translations of Schiller's dramas were presented in other cities of Ontario and Quebec during the later nineteenth century. Readings from his poetry also found an enthusiastic response; particularly popular was his *The Lay of the Bell (Das Lied von der Glocke)* to audiences everywhere. Musical settings of this work, as well as of others of the great German dramatist, continued to be performed regularly in Toronto and elsewhere in Ontario.

In purely German circles the theatrical groups sponsored by the *Turner* societies vied with each other in producing plays, and the German newspapers carried not only the advertising matter inserted by the various *Vereine,* but also commented on the performances, the players, the audience and, in addition, gave words of encouragement and commendation in their columns.

From the very beginning of its existence, the *Canadier* carried a certain amount of poetic and prose literary material. There was a distinct increase in the amount of such matter after Edward Lindemann became editor in October, 1853. The serial story now became a regular feature of the *Canadier.* One of the first such stories was *Die Tochter der Riccarees, Lebensbilder aus Louisiana,* by Friedrich Gerstäcker. It ran for six successive weeks (January 12 to February 16, 1854) and averaged over three full columns per issue. From that time on until the *Canadier's* demise the instalment prose story was a permanent feature. The works of anonymous and relatively unimportant authors are found side by side with the more reputable writers of the period. Among the latter, in addition to Friedrich Gerstäcker, who has already been mentioned, Max Ring, Berthold Auerbach, Louise Mühlbach, Elfried von Taura, Gustav Nieritz, Wilhelm Heinrich Riehl, Franz Hoffman, Alexander Weill, Alfred Meissner and others are represented, many of them by several shorter or longer works. The situation with regard to poetry closely approximates that of the prose. However, more local poets appear than local prose writers. The writing of verse seems to have been considered an easier task than the writing of a prose work. Of the better known German poets the following are represented in the *Canadier:* Friedrich Rückert, Goethe, Friedrich Mathisson, Nikolaus Lenau, Robert Prutz, Ferdinand Freiligrath, Emanuel Geibel, and Hoffmann von Fallersleben. Poetic themes represented vary, with a distinct predilection for the more sentimental effusions of the above writers. The local versifiers often deal with questions of the day, the weather, the seasons, an unusual or tragic event, the palatability of sauerkraut, the transiency of human life, the beauty of the German language, the praise of Canada, and many other topics.

The *Canadier* made some concessions to the local dialect in its everyday vocabulary. A random selection includes words such as "Riegelweg" (Eisenbahn), "Mäpel-Zucker", "Stohr", "Flauer" (flour), and "Klertsche (clergy), Reserven". English news and advertisements are found occasionally though not nearly to the same extent as in the *Canada Museum.* Stylistically the *Canadier* often left much to be desired. This lack of good style and felicitous expression offended the taste of some of the readers, but most of them seem to have been satisfied. Good German was the ideal aimed at, but not always achieved. Otto Klotz of Preston, one of the better educated German immigrants in the community, called attention in August 1845 to the deficiencies in style and language of the *Canadier* and advocated improvement in these departments.

The *Canadier* often disagreed violently with its German contemporaries after it ceased being the only German newspaper serving the German community in 1848. Feuds between rival newspapers were common in the nineteenth century in Ontario, and the German newspapers were no exception. New editors would declare in introducing themselves to the community that they wished to be on friendly terms with their journalistic rivals, but the best of intentions were frequently thwarted, and harsh epithets were often hurled at other editorial heads, as well as at their products. Sometimes the feuds became so acrimonious and were so prolonged that interested individuals outside of the newspaper field intervened, or offered their services, to bring about an armistice in the verbal war. In 1854 a meeting was held at the home of Otto Klotz in Preston, at which Dr. Charles Ebert was the presiding officer, and Julius Meyer the secretary, to discuss ways and means of halting a very bitter verbal conflict between *Der Canadische Beobachter* of New Hamburg and *Der Canadische Bauernfreund* of Preston. The *Canadier* of Berlin was at times involved in feuds with these same newspapers, on which occasions its behaviour could scarcely be viewed as a model of restraint. Typical of the venomous hatred of its competitors is an item of September 9, 1852, directed against the *Beobachter:* "Lost. The last number of the *Hamburger Beobachter* has disappeared from our office. Perhaps someone has used it on the night-stool. That would be in any event the most fitting use that one could make of the *Humbuger rag.*" In fact the *Canadier's* first period of existence came to an end during a violent clash with the *Berliner Journal.*

The *Deutscher Canadier* marked a distinct advance in German journalism in Upper Canada. This advance was evidently inspired by a similar raising of the standard of the German newspapers in the United States through the impact of the Forty-eighters. This group, among which were many intellectuals, was not strongly represented in British North America, although Edward Lindemann, as has been noted, was a Forty-eighter who became the editor of various German weeklies in Upper Canada, including the *Canadier*.

The *Canadier* leaned heavily on its German counterparts in the United States for much of its news and other matter. Among these were the *New Yorker Staatszeitung*, the *Buffalo Weltbürger*, the *Deutsche Schnellpost* of New York, published by Karl Heinzen and J. Tyssowski, the *Alte und neue Welt* of Philadelphia, the *Anzeiger des Westens*, of St. Louis, the *Volksfreund* of Lancaster, Pennsylvania, among others. But English newspapers were also widely used as sources. Here are to be found the Doylestown *Independent Democrat*, the *Buffalo Democrat*, the *Hanover Gazette* (Pennsylvania), the *Philadelphia Minerva*, the Cincinnati *Gazette*, beside the Montreal *Herald*, the *British Colonist*, the Port Hope *Gazette*, the Montreal *Gazette*, the Montreal *Times*, and other Canadian publications.

In its general appearance the *Canadier* made some attempt to vie with the more sprightly German journals south of the border. This necessitated modification from time to time in format.

A combination of circumstances seems to have militated against the continuation of the *Canadier*. It had a number of competitors in the years following 1848, although no serious threat to its existence presented itself until the *Berliner Journal* was established in 1859. The very frequent changes in ownership and the multiplicity of editors it had after 1850 are symptomatic of a lack of stability; the publisher-editor relationships were frequently characterized by a sharp clash of personalities. A struggling venture could not afford the luxury of disputes within its own circle without weakening its vital strength. The most serious blow came, however, in 1859, when Friedrich Rittinger, who had been in charge of the mechanical department of the *Canadier*, left to become the partner of John Motz in the new *Berliner Journal*.

The vigor with which this new rival in Berlin addressed itself to the German community, and its generally aggressive spirit, provided a competition with which the *Canadier*, published in the later years by a non-German, could not cope. It strove hard to maintain itself, but it eventually had to yield the field to its younger and more virile rival.

CHAPTER III
THE FLOURISHING PERIOD, 1850—1900

Toward the end of the fourth and the advent of the fifth decade of the nineteenth century there began a period of feverish activity in the development of the German newspaper press in Ontario. This sudden upsurge coincided with the arrival of the Forty-eighters in America, and reflected the urge that possessed many of their number: to enter the field of journalism. German newspapers began to spring up in a number of the smaller villages in Ontario, and here and there in larger towns, quite frequently in areas where there were not sufficient German-speaking inhabitants to assure any hope of successful operation.

The first of these newcomers was *Der Canadische Beobachter*, which began publication in Preston, near Berlin, in the early months of 1848. Its publisher and editor was Martin Rudolph. The venture proved unsuccessful and after a tenuous existence of approximately two years, Rudolph abandoned it, and sold his printing press to Joseph Erb of Cambridge, near Preston. Erb in turn sold the press to Heinrich Kulp, who had recently arrived in Ontario from Pennsylvania. Kulp, however, found himself unable to raise enough money to make a sufficiently large down-payment on the press and equipment to take full possession. He did, nevertheless, publish a specimen copy, a newspaper edited by himself called the *Prestoner Express*. This specimen copy was so badly edited that Erb was convinced that the *Express* would never find any support, a feeling that was shared in other circles. Erb promptly repossessed his press and gave it to his son, Abraham Erb, who on November 1, 1850, published the first number of *Der Canadische Bauernfreund* in Preston. The *Bauernfreund* supported the Reform party. In appearance it resembled the *Deutscher Canadier*. For some time Martin Rudolph was its editor, but by 1852 he made way for Jakob Teuscher, whose name subsequently was associated for more than twenty years with German newspapers in Ontario.

Rudolph severed his connection with the *Bauernfreund* in order to embark on a new journalistic endeavor of his own. It was again a *Beobachter*, but the locale had shifted from Preston to New Hamburg.

The first number of Rudolph's *Hamburger Beobachter* appeared on January 16, 1852.

The original *Beobachter* in Preston was a four-page weekly, 24 inches high and 21 inches wide, with six columns per page. The shift from Preston to New Hamburg on the part of Rudolph, and the change in name from *Der Canadische Beobachter* to the *Hamburger Beobachter* saw little change in the appearance of the newspaper. The size, however, had been slightly reduced. It was still four pages with six columns per page,

Große Niederlage!!
im
GERMANIA HAUS!
in Berlin.

Clear the
Track !!!

So eben habe ich erhalten die größte und beste Auswahl von

Herbst- und Winterwaaren

bestehend in

Shawls, von jeder Sorte und Größe, Musselins, Merinos, Plaids, Cobourgs, deLaines, 2c. Broadcloths, Doeskins, Satinetts, Flanels,

und überhaupt in jedem Artikel, welcher in die Dry Goodsline einschlägt;

Ferner auch aus

Fertigen Frackröcken, Ueberröcken, Hosen, Kappen und Hüten!

Ebenso halte ich stets vorräthig eine große Auswahl von

Kaffee, Zucker, Thee, Taback, Reis,

so wie von

Eisenwaaren,

Porzellan- und Töpferwaaren, 2c.

Die verschiedenen Sorten Liquors, als:

Pale- und Dark-Brandy, Port-Madeira-Malaga-Weine, Gin, Rum, französischen ächten Cognac, Peppermint, Glasgow-Ale, London Porter,

halte ich von der besten Sorte und guter **Whiskey** wird bei mir sowohl im Großen als auch im Kleinen verkauft.

Vortrefflicher Käse stets vorräthig!

Die Damen aber möchte ich vorzüglich aufmerksam machen auf die schöne Auswahl von

Winterbonnets und Damenmänteln.

Indianrubber- und Lederschuhe in großer Auswahl.

☞ Makrelen, Weißfische, Häringe und andere Fischsorten gepöckelt und trocken! ☜

Indem ich dem Publikum für das mir bisher geschenkte Zutrauen ergebenst danke, darf ich hoffen, daß ich durch Vergrößerung meines Waaren Lagers und größere Mannichfaltigkeit meiner Güter, dasselbe auch ferner zu rechtfertigen im Stande sein, und Niemand meinen Store verlassen werde, ohne befriedigt zu sein.

Schneller Verkauf und kleiner Profit ist mein Grundsatz!

Landwirthschaftliche Produkte werden zum höchsten Marktpreise angenommen.

Unter Zusicherung reeller Bedienung ladet ergebenst ein

John Klein.

Berlin, 7. November, 1854.

but the pages now measured 23 inches high and 19 inches wide. Subscription rates at this time were quoted in English and American currency. Seven shillings and six pence, or one dollar and fifty cents was the subscription price per year if paid in advance or by the end of three months, or two dollars if paid later.

There is a striking similarity in the content of all the German newspapers at this time. The *Beobachter*, whether in Preston or New Hamburg, proved to be no exception. Prose, poetry, foreign, provincial and Canadian news, with little attention to purely local events, characterize the first years of the *Beobachter*. Advertising material was mainly local in origin, and was usually found on pages three and four. The literary prose material in the *Beobachter* was one of its attractive features. Within a period of one year, February 1855 to February 1856, the following authors were represented: Friedrich Gerstäcker by *Der Ostindier* and *Die Nacht auf dem Walfisch;* Gottfried Kinkel by *Der Hauskrieg;* Lermontoff by *Taman;* George Sand by *Melchior;* Dr. A. Douai (a well-known Forty-eighter) by *Der Überfall. Eine Erzählung aus den Zeiten der Republik Texas*, as well as prose by anonymous and lesser-known writers. Included was also a short story by a local writer, John Hinderer, entitled *Trennung und Wiedersehen*. Hinderer later became editor for a short period of the *Canadischer Bauernfreund* after it had moved to Waterloo.

The *Hamburger Beobachter* under Rudolph's direction was a very aggressive newspaper. It reflected the spirit of its editor who was, in some ways, a violent individual. He frequently carried on a running feud with his German journalistic contemporaries, and struck out vehemently at anyone with whom he found himself in disagreement. He could not maintain a neutral position in religion, a characteristic which involved him in endless wrangling and recrimination during the seven years in which he was editor and publisher of the *Beobachter*. But he was also an intelligent and public-spirited citizen whose capabilities found some recognition in his own community. For several years he served as superintendent of the German schools in the New Hamburg area. In this capacity he became, with the cooperation of the German Teachers' Association, the editor and publisher of a short-lived pedagogical journal, *Die Waage*. The first number of this fortnightly, which stood for progress in the fields of religion and education, appeared on April 29, 1853, at a subscription price of fifty cents per year. Its last number probably was issued in February, 1855, as a note in the *Beobachter* of March 2, 1855, states that *Die Waage* has ceased publication.

In May 1854, a new editor was engaged for the *Beobachter* in the person of Franz Joseph Egenter. This was an attempt on the part of Rudolph to stave off the failure of his newspaper, evidences of which were becoming increasingly visible. Egenter had formerly been the editor of the *Seeblätter* in Konstanz, Baden, Germany, and came to the *Beobachter* with some reputation as a poet. His period of service with the *Beobachter* was less than a year. He left to issue a German newspaper, the *Lichtfreund*, in Buffalo after severing his connection with the *Beobachter*.

In February, 1855, George W. Eby became the owner of the *Hamburger*

Beobachter. He brought in Dr. H. Th. Legler, who has been mentioned earlier in regard to his position as editor of the *Canadier*, as editor. The new management took over on March 2, 1855, with the pious hope that it could succeed where Rudolph had failed. It promised to support the Reform party politically; to make its editorial aims those of truth and progress; to adhere to the principle of religious freedom; and to offer entertaining prose material and also instructive articles on agriculture and industry.

On June 3, 1855, George W. Eby sold the *Beobachter* to Peter Eby of Berlin. Dr. Legler retired at the same time as editor. A claim made on July 5, 1855, that the number of subscriptions had increased by five hundred per cent adds nothing materially to our knowledge of the *Beobachter's* situation in this respect, since no definite figures are given.

Martin Rudolph, even after his retirement as owner and editor of the *Beobachter*, found himself in disputes involving violence with individuals and, in addition, ran foul of the law. He was found guilty of blasphemous libel in November 1855 and of assault in January of the following year. The object of his physical violence was Jakob Teuscher, the editor of the *Bauernfreund*. The latter had made what Rudolph considered were slighting remarks about him in the columns of his paper. Rudolph was found guilty and fine nine dollars for this breach of the peace.

The new owner of the *Beobachter*, Peter Eby, tried valiantly to rescue it from failure but unfortunately was not successful. A new competitor in New Hamburg did not improve his position, and the legacy of dissatisfaction left from the Rudolph period made it impossible for him to avoid continuing the local feud. In August 1856 the *Beobachter* suddenly ceased publication.

Although *Der Canadische Beobachter* began its life shortly before the end of the first half of the nineteenth century, its brief existence in Preston was not sufficiently long to establish it as a force in German journalism in Ontario. Its later continuation in New Hamburg, however, gave it a much more dominating position, and as such it belongs primarily to the pioneers of the great flourishing period of the German newspaper press in this province.

From September 1841 to January 1848 the *Deutscher Canadier* of Berlin was the only German newspaper in British North America.

It is interesting to note that the *Canadier's* ownership was, for many years, in the hands of the sons of Bishop Benjamin Eby. The Eby name was also associated with several other Ontario German newspapers. Benjamin Eby had migrated from Pennsylvania to Waterloo County in 1807. He became a Mennonite preacher in 1809, and three years later was elected a bishop of that communion. He was a public-spirited man, and, although his financial resources were never extensive, he gave as generously as his means would permit to every civic enterprise which contributed to the prosperity and advancement of the Waterloo German community. He was also vitally interested in the preservation of the German language in Ontario, and gave tangible evidence of that interest by becoming the first German teacher in the Berlin area. In quarters provided by himself he imparted, with few interruptions, instruction in the German language from 1818 to 1844. In addition he acted as chairman of the German Welfare Society *(Deutsche Wohltätigkeits Gesellschaft)* of Berlin, and was for some years a member of the local school board. For more than forty years Bishop Eby was the district's leading German citizen. He died in 1853 at the age of sixty-eight years.

It was chiefly through Bishop Eby's encouragement and financial support that Henry William Peterson was induced to establish the *Canada Museum* in 1835. The two shares which the Bishop subscribed to this venture were promptly paid. One of Bishop Eby's sons, Heinrich Eby, became Peterson's first apprentice. It was this association by a member of the Eby family with Ontario's pioneer German newspaper which established the printing and publishing tradition in that family. However, Pennsylvania Germans who had migrated to Canada and their descendants, with the exception of several members of the Eby family, took little active part in the history of the Ontario German press.

Before the *Hamburger Beobachter* expired, a new German weekly was initiated in New Hamburg. It bore the name of *Der Neu-Hamburger Neutrale*, and was published by W. H. Boulee and edited by Robert Storch. The first number appeared on January 19, 1855. Storch was a recent immigrant, having been only eight months in America and four weeks in Canada when he undertook his assignment with the new paper. He plunged into his task with pronounced alacrity, and in the prospectus which appeared in the first few issues of the *Neutrale* he radiated a confidence in the venture that was hardly based on the true situation existing in the German areas of Ontario. The tone of this article was somewhat extravagant as well, and scarcely harmonized with the intellectual equipment possessed by the majority of prospective readers of the new weekly [1]. Storch's editorship was of short duration, lasting only until the issue of April 6, 1855. He made a heroic attempt to preserve a neutral attitude, particularly in religion and, to a degree, in politics.

For its size, four pages of five columns each, measuring 23 inches high and 17 inches wide, the *Neutrale* contained a great deal of reading material, as it was printed in a very small size of type. The printing was at all times clear and good with excellent proof-reading. A mistake in spelling was exceedingly rare. The subscription price was one dollar and four shillings per annum if paid within three months, two shillings additional after that period, and two dollars after six months had elapsed. If two numbers were accepted by a person, he was considered to be a subscriber.

The *Neutrale* brought a large volume of news, both foreign and domestic, and chronicled, among other major events during its period of publication, the Crimean War in very detailed fashion for its readers.

There was, as in the other Ontario German newspapers at this period, an almost complete absence of purely local gossip. The German immigrants were in the first phase of their displacement still much more concerned about events in their homeland than in the doings of their new neighbors in the local community where they had taken up their abode. It took some time to fuse a more or less heterogeneous group of people into a well-integrated social unit, in which the internal events assumed a greater importance than certain external ones.

The *Neutrale* carried market prices and local notices of an official nature as a service to its readers. A very considerable bulk of advertising was carried for various and sundry items including lands for sale, auction sales, lost and found, books, apothecary shops, a pottery, many types of patent medicines, harness-makers, doctors' notices, and others. There were many advertisements inserted by people with English names who wished to purvey their wares to the German community.

Serial literary prose was alternated with prose articles in the *Neutrale*. There never was any great bulk of poetry, although Goethe is represented by *Gefunden*, Ferdinand Freiligrath by *Der Blumen Rache*, L. C. H. Hölty by *Elegie*, and Otto Ludwig by *Lied an den Mond* in the initial year. Some anonymous poems, including the works of local poetizers, also appeared during the same period. The prose material, too, was mainly anonymous, or the product of minor writers, although Theodor Meyer-Merian with *Das Gärtlein im Stadtgraben*, Friedrich Gerstäcker with *Die Wolfsglocke*, Josef Rank with *Zu den drei Eichen*, and Ludwig Bechstein with *Der Spielmann vom Thüringer Wald* are all found in the first year of the *Neutrale*.

When Robert Storch resigned his editorship, his duties were taken over by the publisher, W. H. Boullee. Boullee was a man of ability and strong convictions who, under the pressure of criticism and competition eventually forsook the neutral attitude which his newspaper had affirmed in its prospectus, and became embroiled in acrimonious disputes with his German journalistic contemporaries as well as with a Roman Catholic priest of St. Agatha, Pastor Rupert Ebner, S. J. The latter employed the columns of the *Hamburger Beobachter* to carry on his part of the struggle, through which the editor of the *Beobachter* evidently believed some local advantage might accrue to his newspaper. The feud began in consequence of a series of articles under the title of *Die Entwicklungsgeschichte der Hessen*, in the course of which Louis Riedt, a teacher of New Hamburg and their author, made an assertion which offended the religious sensibilities of Pastor Ebner. Boullee conducted his part of the controversy with extraordinary vigor, but the tone of his articles was at times somewhat offensive, although he did not permit himself to descend to the crude personal attacks or the biting satire as was the case when he dealt with his journalistic adversaries. The *Hamburger Beobachter* was a constant object of attack by the *Neutrale*, although this was not a matter of unprovoked aggression. Even former publishers and editors of the *Beobachter*, writhing under misfortune, found the *Neutrale* giving plenty of space to a recital of their dereliction. Thus when Martin Rudolph was found guilty of blasphemous libel against the Christian religion of the realm, or when he lost his position as

Beilage

zum

"Hamburger Beobachter."

Freitag, den 12. Oktober 1855.

Herr Redakteur!

Wenn ich bitten darf, so haben Sie die Güte, folgende Zeilen in ihren Beobachter aufzunehmen. Der sogenannte „Neu-Hamburger Neutrale" hat sich bereits schon seit geraumer Zeit als verächtlichen Partei- und Lügenblatt, und zwar auf dem religiösen Felde, erwiesen. Um Politik scheint sich der fromme Mann allerdings wenig zu bekümmern, aber desto eifriger sucht er auf dem religiösen Gebiete zu fischen, und die Fangnetze der Heuchelei, der Lüge und Verläumdung—zwar auf verschmitzte und verborgene Weise, wie es heuchlerischen und bigotten Muckern eigen ist—dahin u. dorthin auszuwerfen. Die übrigen christlichen Genossenschaften sind zwar bisher verschont geblieben, denn diese glaubt er auf jeden Fall früher oder später unter seinen Hut zu bringen; aber auf die Katholiken soll das Reinigungsbad ausgegossen werden; diese sollen mit dem lieblichen Salböl des Geistes gesalbt und belehrt werden, daß ihre Religion nichts Weiteres als ein Mischmasch von Albernheiten, Betrügereien und Schlechtigkeiten ist. Schon öfters fühlte ich mich versucht, das unehrenhafte Treiben des frommen Redakteurs des Neutralen zu rügen, allein ich dachte mit dem weisen Mann „der Narren Zahl ist endlos" und die Lüge straft sich am Ende selber. Doch vorgestern ward ich auf eine Stelle im Neutralen aufmerksam gemacht, die so kolossale und schamlose Lügen enthält, daß ich nicht umhin kann, dem frechen Lügenmaul mit ein paar Worten entgegenzutreten. Die bezügliche Stelle befindet sich, wie gesagt, im Neutralen vom 7. September, No. 35, in der Entwicklungsgeschichte der Hessen — gleich Anfangs wo es heißt: „Tiefer u. tiefer &c." bis „Schon seit der Mitte des 15. Jahrhunderts &c."

In diesen Sätzen werden folgende fünf Punkte behauptet, und als blanke Wahrheit dem protestantischen wie katholischen Publikum hingestellt:

1) Daß das Fegfeuer eine neue Lehre sei;

2) Daß das Koncilium von Trient nach geologischen Vermessungen (giebt es denn auch geologische Vermessungen?) acht Apartementen (abgesonderte Bezirke) im Fegfeuer für Kaiser, Könige &c. ausgeworfen habe;

3) Daß dasselbe Koncilium acht entsprechende Grade Hitze bestimmt habe;

4) Daß nach dem gleichen Urtheil im Verhältniß zu den acht Graden Hitze eine progressive Besteuerung der Reichen und Großen zur Erzweckung der proportionirten Revenüen der Kirche gebe;

5) Daß endlich nach der Lehre desselben Concils das unterste Apartement stets mit den Seelen der Armen überfüllt sei.

Nun glaube ich, als ein Abonnent des Neutralen ein Recht zu haben, an der geheiligten Pforte desselben um weitere Belehrung anzuklopfen, und an den Redakteur desselben die bescheidene Bitte zu stellen, mir wirklich den Kanon oder das Kapitel des Conciliums von Trient zu citiren, worin die 4 letzten Punkte enthalten und ausgesprochen sind — denn was den ersten Punkt betrifft, nämlich ob das Fegfeuer eine neue Lehre sei, damit will oder kann ich mich vielmehr nicht länger befassen, da die Frage eine rein religiöse ist, der Beobachter aber, als ein politisches Blatt rein religiösen Erörterungen seine Spalten voraussichtlich nicht öffnen wird; so sehr es mir übrigens Freude machen würde, mit dem warmen Bruder vom Neutralen auch hierüber ein paar Worte zu wechseln. Die vier letzten Punkte hingegen sind rein historische Fragen, wobei es sich blos darum handelt, ob das Koncil von Trient selbe gelehrt habe oder nicht. Darüber bitte ich um Aufschluß — erwarte aber Beweise, nicht leere Behauptungen.

Der fromme, des Geistes gewiß übervolle Redakteur des Neutralen wird leicht selbst einsehen, daß es sehr indiskret wäre, diese unschuldige Bitte mir abzuschlagen, die ich nicht blos in meinem, sondern auch in des ganzen katholischen und protestantischen Publikums Interesse stelle; denn ich habe für letzteres zu viel Achtung, als daß ich glauben könnte, daß es für Wahrheit und Lüge gleichgültig sey, oder gar für diese eine Vorliebe habe — und was das erstere betrifft, so wird jeder Katholik mit gespannter Neugierde vernehmen, wie es sich denn eigentlich mit der Lehre des Conciliums von Trient über das Fegfeuer, die acht Apartements, die acht Grad Hitze, die progressive Steuer und die proportionirten Revenüen der Kirche verhalte — lauter Dinge, von denen er bisher keine Sylbe gewußt hat. Ja im eigenen Interesse muß der Redakteur des Neutralen meiner Bitte entsprechen; denn wenn er sich auch noch so groß und heilig fühlt, kann es ihm doch nicht gleichgültig seyn, daß ihn auch nur ein einziger seiner Mitmenschen aus gutem Grunde als einen Verläumder und Verfälscher der Wahrheit ansehen sollte. Und überdieß verspreche ich heilig, wenn die genannten vier Punkte bewiesen werden, daß ich selbst ein Bekehrter und ein warmer Bruder werden will, und daß mein Beispiel gewiß viele Nachfolger finden wird; werden die Beweise aber nicht gebracht, dann mag sich der warme Bruder vom Neutralen mit seiner Belehrung zum schwarzen Kaspar scheeren, damit ihm in seiner Gesellschaft noch wärmer werde, ja heißer werde, als es in den acht fraglichen Apartments zusammen ist; auch erkläre ich in diesem Falle den Redakteur wie auch seinen Geschichtschreiber vor dem ganzen Publikum ein für alle Mal für infame Lügner, schamlose Verläumder, fanatische Dunkelköpfe und bigotte Schurken, die gewissenlos genug sind, ohne die mindeste Veranlassung und ohne den mindesten Grund das religiöse Gefühl ihrer Mitbürger auf das boshafteste zu verletzen, und die zahlreichste Klasse der Bekenner des christlichen Glaubens mit dem Geifer ihres Zelotenthums zu bewerfen.

P. Rupert Ebner, S. J.

St. Agatha, 24. Sept. 1855.

---

* Wir konnten diesen Artikel nicht in unser Blatt aufnehmen, da er in demselben zu viel Raum eingenommen hätte; betrachten es aber als unsere Pflicht, denselben zu veröffentlichen, um den Angegriffenen Gelegenheit zu geben, sich zu vertheidigen. (D. Red. d. Beob.)

station master in Preston, the *Neutrale* brought a full report, although many other local items of importance were overlooked. Similarly, when Joseph Egenter, formerly editor of the *Beobachter*, and subsequently publisher and editor of the Buffalo *Lichtfreund*, had to suspend publication of that paper, not a note of sympathy at his unhappy fate is found in the *Neutrale*.

A feud with the *Prestoner Zeitung*, too, went on in 1857. The *Zeitung* was later forced into bankruptcy. Its existence was, on one occasion the butt of a satiric dialogue between two unidentified characters, Schulze and Miller; its demise evoked no sympathy; and the departure of its former editor, Friedrich Keller, to the United States elicited only a jeering remark from Boullee. Boullee himself eventually left Canada in 1878, presumably to escape from his creditors, who promptly sold his chattels in order to recover, at least partially, any loss they might have sustained.

The *Neutrale* was an ardent advocate of German language study, and frequently gave encouragement to this pursuit in its columns. It also supported the *Hamburger Turn- und Sängerverein* although not without a carping undertone at times.[2] Information about Canada was always brought to enlighten the new immigrants as to the country's geography, products, climate, soil, its educational and political system. The *Neutrale* in this way made a distinct contribution to the introduction of the Germans into the Canadian pattern.

The *Neutrale* never gave any hint as to the size of its subscription list after April 6, 1855. In the issue of that day it recorded the names and addresses of 109 paid subscribers from various parts of the German-speaking area in Ontario. It must be assumed that its subscription list was never large. It did, however, find excellent advertising support, and that not only from German sources. Neither were the advertisements mainly of local origin. We may guess from this situation that the *Neutrale* was relatively widely, if not heavily, distributed.

In 1859, with the beginning of its fifth volume, the *Neu-Hamburger Neutrale* was taken over by George Reynolds, as publisher and editor, and its name changed to the *Canadisches Volksblatt*. Under this title it appeared regularly in New Hamburg until December 2, 1908, when it was merged with the *Canadischer Bauernfreund* in Waterloo. Its last publisher, Daniel Ritz, remained as its agent in New Hamburg.

In rapid succession two more German newspapers made their appearance in the middle of the 1850's, only to fade into oblivion after very short periods of publication. The first of these was the *Canada Zeitung*, published in Hamilton, Upper Canada, with Ludwig Krause as editor. It was a small sheet, issued twice weekly, the first number appearing in January 1856. Almost immediately differences arose between the sponsors of the venture and the editor, with the result that the latter was dismissed on March 24, 1856, after having held his position for only eleven numbers. An attempt to put this paper on a more solid footing, with Ch. Pfeiffer as publisher, failed, and the *Canada Zeitung* disappeared in August 1857.

"Selig sind Die, welche nicht bezahlen.
Denn sie brauchen keine Quittungen aufzuheben."
Hier ruhet die schmerzliche Hülle des schmerzlichen
HERRN C.F.F. KAYSER
Schmerzlicher Redakteur
Marktplatze in Berlin, am 7. Sept. 1865, Morgens halb 10 Uhr aus.
Eifer-Gelb- und galoppirender Schwindsucht
sein geistiges Vermögen verlor.

The second German weekly to begin publication in 1856 was *Die Prestoner Zeitung*, in the village of Preston, with Peter G. Gefrörer as publisher, and Friedrich Keller as editor. The initial number appeared in November 1856. It was published every Thursday with a subscription rate of two dollars per annum, or one dollar and fifty cents if paid within three months. After one year the *Prestoner Zeitung* also failed. Peter Gefrörer later became publisher of the *Banner* in Terre Haute, Indiana.

In the midst of these failures the *Deutscher Canadier* of Berlin, and *Der Canadische Bauernfreund und Allgemeine Anzeiger für Waterloo County* of Waterloo maintained themselves. The *Bauernfreund*, as the latter was usually called, was a four-page weekly, 24 inches high and 18 inches wide, with six columns per page. It was well edited and carefully printed and, in general appearance, was not dissimilar from its other German contemporaries. Its yearly subscription rate was two dollars, half-yearly one dollar, in both instances in advance. This was later changed to one dollar and fifty cents in advance, or two dollars if paid after six months.

Preston, where the *Bauernfreund* was originally established, was in 1850 the largest village in Waterloo Township. The village of Waterloo contained about 250 inhabitants; Berlin, as has been noted, about 750; Preston about 1100. W. H. Smith, in his *Canada: Past, Present and Future*, has the following to say about this village: "Preston contains about eleven hundred inhabitants, principally Germans ... An agricultural paper, *Canadische (sic) Bauernfreund, or Canadian Farmer's Friend*, is published in Preston."

However, the *Bauernfreund* remained in Preston only during the first few years of its existence. In 1854 it was bought by Moses Springer, who moved it to the village of Waterloo. Here it stayed for the remainder of its life. Jakob Teuscher was retained by Springer in the move to continue his editorial duties with the paper. The *Bauernfreund* passed in quick succession through the hands of several owners before Joachim Kalbfleisch and Hartmann Schnarr purchased it in 1860. Teuscher remained as editor; Schnarr soon sold his share to Kalbfleisch, who from that time on was sole owner. After Teuscher left to found the *Kolonist* in Stratford in 1863, John Hinderer became editor for a time. Hinderer, who was born in Oberdorf, Oberamt Welzheim, Königreich (Kingdom of) Württemberg, had migrated to the United States in 1852. He came to Canada in 1855 and died in 1865, evidently of tuberculosis, at the age of thirty-eight years. A man of literary capabilities, he wrote both prose and poetry with some distinction. At his funeral in June 1865 the *Turner* sang a dirge written and composed by him, entitled: *Ruhe sanft im Schoß der kühlen Erde.*

After Hinderer's death a Berlin bookbinder, C. C. F. Kayser, became the editor of the *Bauernfreund*. Kayser was an enthusiastic local poet who had frequently been given space, as well as encouragement, in the columns of the *Berliner Journal* before he moved to his editorial position in Waterloo. He also contributed to Adolph Pressprich's *Deutsch-Canadische Familienblätter*, issued in New Hamburg in 1865. After joining the *Bauernfreund* in the late summer of 1865 Kayser almost immediately became involved in a dispute with his former friends in Berlin, and harsh words were exchanged in this feud between the *Journal* and the *Bauernfreund.* However, it did not last long as he resigned his editorship in November 1865 and left Canada. His departure was marked by a scathing broadside, whose authorship cannot now be established, but our surmise must be that it originated in a certain Berlin newspaper office. It read as follows:

Blessed are those who
do not pay their bills
for they do not have to
preserve any receipts.

Here rest the agonized remains of the agonized Mr. C. C. F. Kayser, the agonized editor of the agonized friend of the agonized farmers in Waterloo, who was never a book-binder, vitalizer, woodcarver, poet, etc., etc.
The same breathed out his noble soul on the market-place in Berlin, September 7, 1865, at 9:30 in the morning.
Medical investigation revealed that the memorable one lost his mental resources as the result of jealousy, jaundice, and galloping consumption. The dear fellow died as he lived; his last sigh was vouchsafed the rump steaks of the many slaughtered offerings at the market in Berlin, which sang a dismal dirge to him.

The deceased left his imperial, but nevertheless sad, career without friends; the businessmen of the immediate area lose, moreover, in the departed one, their best customer, as he always had an extraordinary appetite and a terrific thirst. As a result he held in high regard children's parties with cake, picnics with beer, coffee hours with women friends, sausage sampling with double-strength caraway liqueur, etc., etc.
When his last will, whose executor is the agonized capmaker Schade, was read, it was discovered that the noble gentleman, according to section 13, had willed his excellent appetite to the agonized Mr. W. Fischer; and according to section 14, his terrific thirst to the agonized J. Schuh of Waterloo; another clause forbids the aforementioned heirs to visit the Berlin market; consequently the Berlin innkeepers need not become excited.

Peace be to his imperial ashes

To Jakob Teuscher, who had become associated with the *Bauernfreund* soon after it was founded in Preston in 1850, must go a great share of the credit for the firm establishment of this newspaper. For a short period of time before Kalbfleisch and Schnarr purchased it, Teuscher was its owner as well as its editor. For some time, too, the printing press on which the *Bauernfreund* was printed was owned by Caspar Hett, who later turned up again in connection with a short-lived German newspaper in Berlin in the 1880's.

Joachim Kalbfleisch had, previous to his taking over of the *Bauernfreund,* been associated with the *Deutscher Canadier* in Berlin as a printer. Subsequently he was a journeyman printer in Rochester, New York; Peoria, Illinois; and finally in Davenport, Iowa. It was in the latter city that he met John Motz, later editor of the *Berliner Journal.* The two men decided to return to Canada in the autumn of 1857. Their ambition was to become publishers or editors of German newspapers in the Waterloo County area. Both men realized their wishes, Motz a few months earlier than Kalbfleisch. Kalbfleisch was known as an indefatigable worker who found time, however, in addition to his editorial duties, to enter with great fervor into the musical life of the village of Waterloo. In politics he was a Conservative and vigorously supported that party in the columns of the *Bauernfreund*.

The *Bauernfreund* again represented a distinct advance in German newspaper publishing in Ontario. To good presentation of all types of matter must be ascribed its ability to survive in the German community. Kalbfleisch knew the value of advertising his own product and did so when the opportunity presented itself, even in English publications. He claimed a subscription list of over 1000 in a full-page advertisement in *Sutherland's Gazetteer for 1870—71.*[3] Another source gives a circulation of over 1000 to the *Bauernfreund* in 1884.[4]

In appearance the *Bauernfreund* may be compared to the *Berliner Journal*, its contemporary in Berlin. Two columns of advertising usually adorned the first page, flanked by a *feuilleton*. The serial story was heavily represented under this rubric. Foreign, Canadian, and local happenings were well covered, with a preponderance of political news. The balance between advertising and other features was judiciously maintained. A typical number (May 14, 1868) has fourteen columns of advertising out of a total of thirty-two columns. Good print and careful editing were a continued feature of the *Bauernfreund*.

Although Kalbfleisch was a strong advocate of German language study in the schools, and of the retention of German customs, particularly of German song, he nevertheless was firmly attached to the land of his adoption. Born in Eulersdorf bei Grebenau, in Hessen-Darmstadt, Germany, in 1836, he had come to Canada at the age of twelve years. He served first as an apprentice on the *Canadischer Beobachter* under Martin Rudolph in Preston. It was the failure of this paper which forced him to seek employment elsewhere, including various places in the United States. His connection with the *Bauernfreund* lasted for forty-three years, thirty-eight of which he served both as publisher and editor. He died in Waterloo Village in April 1903, at the age of sixty-seven years.

In August 1903, several months after Kalbfleisch's death, the *Bauernfreund* passed into the hands of the *Deutsche Druck- und Verlag-Gesellschaft* of Berlin. The *Deutsche Zeitung*, which had ceased publication some years earlier, was revived and amalgamated with the *Bauernfreund*. Andreas Weidenhammer, a teacher in the public school in Waterloo Village, became the editor of the combined weeklies. Weidenhammer was born at Heidelberg, Ontario, in 1863, and died as Andrew Willows in Manitoba, where he had become an inspector of schools, in 1925. Before leaving Waterloo in 1909, he served as a member of its town council and later as its mayor.

A period of rapid expansion in the *Bauernfreund's* circulation ensued after 1903. By 1905 the subscription list stood at 1625; in 1906 it was 2175. It hovered around this mark until the end of its existence. The amalgamation with the *Deutsche Zeitung* resulted in no increase in price. It remained at one dollar and fifty cents per annum for the eight-page paper, which measured at this time 17 inches wide and 22 inches high.

On July 1, 1909, the *Bauernfreund* passed into the hands of Rittinger and Motz of the *Berliner Journal*. It was the last of the then existing German newspapers outside of Berlin to amalgamate with the *Journal*. The *Bauernfreund* had already previously, on December 2, 1908, assimilated the *Canadisches Volksblatt* of New Hamburg and was in a flourishing state when it discontinued its own independent existence.

The first number of the *Berliner Journal*, the German newspaper which was to assume the dominant role in the field of German journalism in the province, appeared on December 29, 1859, in Berlin. The beginnings of this newspaper were indeed modest, but the optimism of the two founders as to the ultimate success of their venture is apparent on every page of the *Journal* from its initial number.

The augury of this success lay to a great extent in the congenial partnership of two men, John Motz and Friedrich Rittinger, who, although of different religious persuasions, viewed all other problems which faced their cooperative undertaking with an undivided mind. Friedrich Rittinger was born on December 6, 1833, in Michelbach, Grand Duchy of Baden, Germany. In the company of his father, two brothers and one sister, he came to Canada in 1847. After brief stays in Cornwall and Morrisburg, the Rittinger family moved to Berlin in 1848. Friedrich almost immediately became an apprentice in Heinrich Eby's printing establishment, in which at this time the *Deutscher Canadier* was being published. This business went into the hands of Peter Eby, who founded the *Berlin Telegraph*, the first English newspaper to be published in Berlin, Ontario, the initial number of which appeared on January 7, 1853.

In 1859 Rittinger left the *Canadier* to enter into partnership with John Motz on the new *Berliner Journal*. To it he brought a high degree of technical skill to match his partner's facile pen. For thirty-eight years, until Rittinger's death on October 12, 1897, these two men guided the destinies of the *Journal*. Their sons were to carry on where they left off.

Rittinger was a member of the Lutheran Church, but his membership in this confession did not exclude an abundant toleration of other denominations.

Four children and his widow survived him when he died. One of his sons, John A. Rittinger, became the editor and publisher of the *Ontario Glocke* in Walkerton; two other sons, William and Herman, were on the staff of the *Journal*. The surviving daughter was the wife of a Lutheran minister, Pastor Julius Badke.

John Motz, Rittinger's partner, was born in Diedorf bei Mühlhausen, Thuringia, Germany, on June 5, 1830, and came to Waterloo, Upper Canada, in June 1848. He worked for several years as a farm hand and shingle cutter, and later served as an apprentice to C. K. Nahrgang, a tailor, for a period of three years. He carried on a business of his own in Petersburg and St. Jacobs for a short time, and then spent a year in Davenport, Iowa, and Rock Island, Illinois. It was while on his travels that he met Joachim Kalbfleisch. The two men decided to return to

Waterloo County, Canada West, in order to explore the opportunities for making a livelihood there.

Motz returned to Berlin in 1858 and entered the local grammar school with the intention of preparing himself for a teaching career, although he was then over twenty-seven years of age. The resolution to enter the teaching profession, however, was abandoned as the result of his friendship with Friedrich Rittinger who by this time was an expert printer. It was then that the thought ripened in them to publish a German newspaper. They concluded that it would be more advantageous to acquire a well-established paper and consequently negotiated for the purchase of the *Deutscher Canadier*. The owner of the latter, however, refused to sell, which necessitated the projection of the *Berliner Journal*. Of this newspaper Motz became, and remained, editor for forty years.

In addition to his editorial duties, John Motz found time to play a leading part in the life of the community. His public spirit soon drew him into the political arena. He was also a member of the High School and Public Library boards as well as president of the Reform Association of North Waterloo. Following his retirement as editor of the *Journal* in 1899, he was appointed sheriff of Waterloo County, an office which he held until his death in 1911.

Motz was an ardent Reformer in politics and a devout Roman Catholic in religion. At no time, however, is there to be found in him any vestige of religious intolerance toward those of other faiths.

The circumstances surrounding the *Journal's* advent were humble indeed. The German types were secured from Joseph Unzicker, of Hamilton, by payment of a promissory note against Unzicker's *Katholisches Wochenblatt*, which had just suspended publication, after approximately two years of unsuccessful operation.[5] The type for the first number was set in the house of Friedrich Rittinger, approximately at the corner of Queen and Weber Streets in present-day Kitchener. The hand press of the *Berlin Chronicle*, an English newspaper in Berlin, was used to print the initial number. The *Chronicle* office also served for some time as the *Journal* office. The first number was sent to six hundred subscribers and prospective subscribers. The subsequent story of the *Journal* was one of steady growth and expansion.

The dozen years following the establishment of the *Berliner Journal* were again very active years in the history of German journalism in Ontario.

The *Neu-Hamburger Neutrale*, the stormy petrel of German journalism in Waterloo County, had come into new hands by 1859. Under the direction of its new editor and publisher, George Reynolds, it began a more tranquil existence. Printed in very fine type, the *Canadisches Volksblatt*, as it was now called, carried correspondingly more material in its four pages than most of the other Ontario German weeklies. Its annual subscription price at this time was two dollars, or one dollar for six months. Its page size was 22 inches high, and 18 inches wide, with seven columns of print per page. Reynolds also did book and job printing in addition to his newspaper work.

1871. 1871.

Glückwunsch zum Neujahr

der Träger des

„Canadisches Volksblatt."

Das Canadische Volksblatt

Jährlicher Abonnementspreis $1.50 im Voraus,

oder $2.00 am Ende des Jahres.

Wand- und Office-Kalender.

Deutsche und englische

Buch- und Accidenz-Druckerei,

Neu-Hamburg, Ont.

Frequent changes in ownership characterize the life of the *Volksblatt*, which continued to exist until December, 1908, when it was sold to the *Bauernfreund* in Waterloo. George Reynolds published it until 1862 when it was purchased by Samuel Merner (later Senator Merner). In 1864 Merner sold it to Otto Pressprich who became its sole owner in January, 1865. Pressprich had already served as editor and publisher of the *Volksbaltt* since the beginning of 1863. In 1871 Jakob Ritz became Pressprich's partner. This partnership continued until 1884 when Otto Pressprich, who had been associated for more than twenty years as editor as well as owner and part-owner for some of that time, retired from the paper, and Jakob Ritz and Company took over at the beginning of 1885, with Charles (Carl F. H.) Metzdorf as editor. In 1891 Pressprich moved to Sebewaing, Michigan, after living for thirty-four years in New Hamburg. He died at Port Huron, Michigan, in 1896, at the age of sixty-three years. He had come to Canada in 1856 from Grossenhain, Kingdom of Saxony.

In 1892 Daniel Ritz became sole owner of the paper when he took over the business from Jakob Ritz and Company. This arrangement lasted until September 1895, when the *Volksblatt* came into the hands of the *Hamburg Druckgesellschaft*, headed by Otto E. Pressprich, the son of Otto Pressprich. After two and a half years Pressprich resigned his position which was taken by George Rinner, who had been foreman for approximately ten years in the *Ontario Glocke* printing office in Walkerton. Rinner, who had begun his printing career as a type-setter on the *Volksblatt*, remained, however, only from April to December of 1898 in this position. Daniel Ritz was the last publisher of the *Volksblatt*.

The *Canadisches Volksblatt* experienced its flourishing period during the editorship and general direction of Otto Pressprich. He experimented with various page sizes and numbers of columns per page and eventually enlarged the *Volksblatt* to eight pages with six columns per page. That Pressprich was a vigorous man is attested to by his manifold activities. In addition to his editorial duties on the *Volksblatt* he assisted his brother, Adolph Pressprich, for some time in the publishing of the *Deutsch-Canadische Familienblätter*, a monthly German journal of sixteen pages containing poems, novels, short stories and other miscellaneous material, as well as being the printer and publisher of *Das Kirchenblatt*, the official organ of the Evangelical Lutheran Synod of Canada. He was also active in the theatre of the *Turnverein*, functioning as stage director for several years. On February 28, 1865, *Hedwig, die Banditenbraut*, a drama in three acts by Theodor Körner, was given under his direction. In that same month the first number of the *Deutsch-Canadische Familienblätter* appeared. He also served as reeve of New Hamburg in 1882.

A *Turner* society was very active in New Hamburg and received excellent support from the *Volksblatt*. It had been established in 1863, and immediately threw itself vigorously into theatrical work. The *Volksblatt* carried the regular advertising material of the *Verein* and also gave much free publicity in its columns to all activities of this organization. It quite evidently saw in it an instrument for the retaining of interest in the German stage, and the fostering of interest in German customs generally. Its wider implications also comprehended interest in the German newspapers, which to Pressprich, as well as to other German editors and publishers, was of more than academic concern.

The *Turner* societies made some attempt to provide liaison between the various German communities, even beyond the borders of Canada. *Turner* celebrations held in Preston, New Hamburg, Waterloo or Berlin would draw participants from Buffalo, Detroit, Toronto, and Hamilton. Or the local *Turners* would visit those towns and cities where the dramas of A. von Kotzebue, Carl von Holtei, H. Börnstein, K. A. Görner, L. Schneider, L. S. Mercier, L. Feldmann and others were presented in the dramatic offerings of the *Turner* theatre. Occasionally the *Volksblatt* issued a plaintive note that the *Turnvereine* were disappearing, although the one in Preston seems to have retained its vigor when others foundered. The *Volksblatt* advertised a theatrical performance by the Preston *Turners* to be given on December 27, 1869. The piece was Kotzebue's *Verkleidungen*. It also gave considerable space to the celebration of the eighteenth anniversary of the same *Verein*, which took place on September 12, 1872.

The *Volksblatt* usually ran its prose fiction on the first page, followed by local items and European news on page two. Page three contained any surplus news items from page two, supplemented by advertising matter. In the four-page period the last page had mainly advertisements, with a section on useful items for the farmer and town dweller and occasionally some miscellaneous material on all imaginable subjects. The advertising material included the usual run of items to be found, not only in German, but also in English newspapers in Ontario at this time. There were advertisements for books — in this case, German — stores, hotels, ship companies, doctors, newspapers — quite often American — and most voluminous and flamboyant of all: patent medicines. There were also official notices and reports of court proceedings.

The *Volksblatt* was just as intent on providing belletristic material in both prose and poetry as its neighboring German competitors. Intermingled with anonymous writers and those of passing significance we find Theodor Storm represented by *Auf der Universität*, Alfred de Vigny with *Der rothe Siegel*, and Fanny Lewald with *Die Hausgenossen* in the years 1885 and 1886. Translated novels and short stories by American and English authors were also popular in the *Volksblatt*, as indeed with all German newspapers in Ontario. Poetry, too, was often translated from English and appeared side by side with the English original. Grouped in one issue we might find *Sonntags am Rhein* by Ferdinand Freiligrath, with *Der Zauber der Heimath* adapted from Felicia Hemans by Freiligrath. The *Volksblatt* did not offer as great a quantity of poetry as some of its German contemporaries in its earlier period but about the same amount of literary prose.

The bulk of literary material was, however, substantially increased in the later period. Between 1890 and 1895 the following poets are represented: Hermann Lingg, Heinrich Seidel, J. P. Hebel, Ernst von Wolzogen,

A. Fitger, Goethe, Prinz Emil zu Schönaich-Carolath, Gottfried Keller, Friedrich Bodenstedt, Wilhelm Jensen, Felix Dahn, Ludwig Fulda, Droste-Hülshoff, Freiligrath, Rudolf Baumbach, Johannes Trojan, Gustav Falke, Robert Prutz, Theodor Körner, Eduard Dorsch (a prominent Forty-eighter), Karl Gerok, Emanuel Geibel, Ludwig Uhland and Karl Simrock. In addition to poems by these more renowned writers during the above period, there is also a good representation of the works of mediocre and anonymous poetizers. During the same period serial prose is represented by *Gift und Gegengift, Truggeister*, and *Der Scharffenstein*, all by Anton Freiherr von Perfall; *Hans Jochems Brautfahrt* by Adelheid von Rothenburg; *Der Weg zum Glück* by H. v. Osten; *Nach Standrecht* by C. Spielmann; *Der Lohmeier* by Hans Buschmann; *Das Schicksal* by Friedrich Jacobson; *Der jüngste Bruder*, a social novel by Ernst Wichert; *Der Zigeunerbaron* by Moritz Jokai; *Der Afrikareisende* and *Ohne Gewissen* by Reinhold Ortmann; *Ein Gottesurtheil* by Elizabeth Werner; *Himmel und Hölle* by Leopold v. Sacher-Masoch; *Der Klosterjäger* by Ludwig Ganghofer; *Vor den Schranken* by Ernst von Wildenbruch; *Lumpenmüllers Lieschen* by B. Heimburg; *Vor hundert Jahren* by Woldemar Urban; and *Eine Tochter des Südens*, a novel adapted from the French by Friedrich Regensberg. In addition to these longer literary works there were also frequent short sketches, both of a serious and humorous nature. The *Volksblatt* provided only a very scanty quantity of matter in the local dialect or in Pennsylvania German, although there was an increase in this type of material after 1895. New Hamburg and its immediate vicinity had been settled largely by immigrants directly from Germany and consequently there were fewer readers who required to be satisfied by being provided with dialect matter.

In politics the *Volksblatt* was, except during the period of Otto Pressprich's editorship, uncompromisingly Conservative. To the cause of this party it gave fervent editorial and advertising support during the last twenty-five years of its existence. The return of a Liberal government in the federal election of 1896 was interpreted by the *Volksblatt* as an affront to the memory of that great Canadian Conservative statesman, Sir John A. Macdonald, whose passing in 1891 it had marked by profuse and spacious eulogies.

Some circulation figures are available for the *Volksblatt*. According to them it had an estimated number of 820 subscribers in 1873, 1000 in 1877, and not more than 1000 in 1884. By 1906 its subscription list had increased to 1250, which number dropped to 1100 in 1908, the year in which it suspended publication.

The *Volksblatt* was always carefully printed in clean, legible type. Its success in satisfying its patronage is indicated by the length of its existence — almost fifty years. And that in the presence of strong competition from German contemporaries on both sides — in Stratford on the west, and in Berlin and Waterloo in the east. These towns were fewer than twenty miles away from New Hamburg. The *Volksblatt* was German and Canadian in spirit at the same time. It was not deserving of a caustic criticism levelled in particular against it, as well as in

NEW FALL GOODS!

The subscribers beg to inform the inhabitants of Berlin and County of Waterloo, that they will in a course of a few days open out in

FUCHS' BLOCK, BERLIN,

with an entirely NEW AND CAREFULLY SELECTED STOCK OF

STAPLE AND FANCY DRY GOODS,

imported directly for themselves, and which they feel confident will on inspection be found fully lower than any goods that have been brought into the County of Waterloo by any previous importer.

THE AMERICAN & CANADIAN MANUFACTURED GOODS,

comprising all the well known brands of COTTONS and WOOLEN, having been purchased by them for NET CASH will be found in every way up to, and beyond, any goods, heretofore offered.

They purpose selling their goods

CHEAP FOR CASH OR PRODUCE,

which will enable them to offer great inducements to close buyers; and the Motto of small profits and quick returns will be adhered to.

They kindly invite an inspection of their goods before intending buyers will purchase elsewhere, so as they might see for themselves the BARGAINS that would be laid out before them.

NO TROUBLE TO SHEW GOODS.

FRASER, KAISER & Co.

Berlin, September 12, 1871

Neue Herbst-Waaren!

Die Unterzeichneten erlauben sich, die Einwohner von Berlin und dem County Waterloo anzuzeigen, daß sie in einigen Tagen in

Fuchs' Block, Berlin,

ein ganz neues und sorgfältig gewähltes Lager von

Stapel- und Fancy-Ellen-Waaren!!

direkt für sie importirt, eröffnen werden, und sie sind überzeugt, daß man bei Besichtigung ihre Waaren viel billiger finden wird, als irgend welche, die je zuvor in das County Waterloo gebracht wurden.

Ihre amerikanischen und canadischen Fabrikate,

enthaltend alle gutbekannten Sorten **Baumwollen- und Wollenwaaren,** sind für **Baargeld** eingekauft worden und werden in jeder Beziehung alle seither hier feilgebotenen Waaren übertreffen.

Sie beabsichtigen, ihre Waaren

Billig für Baargeld oder Produkte zu verkaufen

und sind daher im Stande, genauen Käufern große Vortheile zu offeriren. Das Motto: Kleiner Profit und schneller Umsatz, wird befolgt werden.

Sie bitten höflichst um Besichtigung ihrer Waaren, bevor man sonstwo einkauft, so daß man selbst beurtheilen kann, welche Vortheile sie den Käufern bieten.

Keine Mühe, Waaren zu zeigen.

Fraser, Kaiser und Co.

Berlin, 12. September 1871.

general against all the other German newspapers in Ontario, by Karl Müller-Grote, a German who spent some years in Berlin, Ontario, during the closing decades of the nineteenth century, and who returned to Germany some time before the outbreak of the first World War. According to this critic, there existed a striking incongruity between external form and inner content of the *Volksblatt*, and that a readable leading article in the German newspapers of Ontario was a rarity, and that in any event it would have been out of keeping with the modest intellectual requirements of their clientèle. According to him, local gossip filled many columns every week. In addition the advertising material, supposedly in literal rendition from English prototypes, was written in such a distorted German as to inspire the reader either to mirth or anger.[6]

It is not difficult to refute Müller-Grote's criticism. While it is true that in the last twenty years of their existence the German newspapers in Ontario laid more emphasis on local gossip than previously, this feature absorbed only a very small part of the total space. Nor is his comment on the German style of the advertisements valid. Though there may have been some influence in that quarter from the English newspapers, a fairly good standard of German was maintained in the advertising material. Since the German newspapers frequently printed advertising material in English, it would be more correct to say that their English advertisements demonstrated a more or less literal rendition of the German originals.

The *Volksblatt*, in common with the other German newspapers of Ontario, made a substantial and determined effort to raise the general standard of education among its German patronage. But with the exception of a small sprinkling of professional men who had migrated to Canada, the clientèle of the German papers was composed largely of farmers, artisans and shopkeepers. Since the latter groups were by far in the majority, it was to these that the newspapers, for practical reasons, had to address themselves. But it would be unjust and misleading to claim that they lacked a high ideal, even though they may often have fallen short of it.

Canadian events consistently received copious coverage. The confederation proceedings, the Red River Rebellion, the Fenian raids, Canada's participation in the Boer War, John A. Macdonald and his National Policy, and other events of the period were kept before its clientèle. International events, such as the Franco-Prussian War and the Russo-Japanese War of 1904—1905 were just as fully reported. Canada's relations with the United States were a frequent subject. A special article of March 6, 1889, by Professor Jacob Gould Schurman, Professor of Philosophy at Cornell University, Ithaca, New York, rejecting the idea of Canada joining, or being annexed by, the United States has not lost its timeliness even in our day, Professor Schurman, who was born in Prince Edward Island, later became president of Cornell University, and after the first World War served as American ambassador to Germany.

The assassination of President William McKinley of the United Staates was reported in detail in the issues of September 11 and 18, 1901.
Whenever a public event had German overtones it received particularly sympathetic treatment in the *Volksblatt*. The centenary of Alexander von Humboldt's birth was celebrated on September 13 and 14, 1869, in Detroit. The exploits of this renowned German scientist and geographer were lauded and an invitation was extended to local admirers of Humboldt to attend this event. When the German-Canadians of Western Ontario decided to form a *Deutsch-Canadischer Nationalverein* at Mildmay, Ontario, on November 8, 1871, the *Volksblatt* warmly applauded this move. John Klein became president and Victor Lang a member of the Central Commitee of this German-Canadian National Union. These two men both played a part in German journalism. That the above organization took an active interest in the cause of German-Canadianism is evident from an article of February 7, 1872, which recounted a visit to Toronto by Messrs. Klein and Lang in the interests of German-English schools in Ontario. It was recorded that they received a favorable reception from Premier Edward Blake and the provincial Superintendent of Education, Egerton Ryerson.
The *Volksblatt* was vitally interested in instilling strong patriotism not only in its German readers to their adopted Canada, but in Canadians of every origin.[7] That the Germans were particularly loyal to His Majesty King Edward VII was, according to the editor, a sign of gratitude for having found a haven in a country where free British institutions flourished.[8] But the *Volksblatt* never wavered in its support of German customs and language in America.[9] It advocated a particularly bold defiance of the nativist, and expressed complete contempt for the German who refused to speak his beautiful mother tongue in Canada.[10]
On June 6, 1863, a four-page German newspaper, published and edited by Jakob Teuscher as volume one, number one, was issued in the village of Waterloo. It was 20 inches high, 14 inches wide and had five columns per page. Its name was *Der Deutsche Reformer*, and it was printed in the office of the Waterloo *Chronicle*, an English newspaper. The editor outlined his program in this, his first number. He noted that it would be at that juncture the sixth German newspaper in Waterloo county, and that it intended to enter the ranks as a champion of reform and independence. He promised to combat the suppression of the truth and to present facts simply so that the common man might understand the issues, in whatever field they might lie. Religion and the church were to enter discussion only in so far as they had political implications. The subscription price of the *Reformer* was one dollar per annum in advance.

The contents of this newspaper were made up of political news and were in effect nothing less than a strong attempt to persuade German voters to cast their ballots for Reform candidates, who were highly lauded, in the forthcoming elections. There was a sharp attack on the *Canadischer Bauernfreund* of Waterloo for its espousal of the Conservative party.

The print was excellent and varied between Latin and German type. Out of the twenty columns in the *Reformer*, six and a half were in good-sized Latin type.

It seems that only a few numbers of this newspaper were ever issued, and it must be assumed that Teuscher, whose political sympathies were on the Reform side and who therefore disagreed with Kalbfleisch of the *Bauernfreund*, which newspaper had favored the Reformers under Teuscher's editorship, was induced in *Der Deutsche Reformer* to break a lance in the cause of his old friends. Before the end of 1863 Teuscher moved to Stratford in order to prepare for the founding of *Der Canadische Kolonist* in that town.

Jakob Teuscher, as has been noted, removed to Stratford in the autumn of 1863 to begin the publishing of the first German newspaper outside Waterloo County. By 1860 the German population had spilled over into the surrounding counties of Perth and Huron, and toward the north into Grey and Bruce. While Waterloo County continued to be looked upon as the focal point of German settlement, solid German communities in the surrounding counties were numerically strong enough to support a German newspaper. Teuscher set out in response to this situation to address himself particularly to the Germans in Perth and Huron. His original intention was to name the new paper *Die Freie Presse*, and under that name issued a prospectus in the *County of Perth Gazetteer for 1863-64*, outlining the policies this newspaper would follow.[11] However, before the first issue of Teuscher's paper appeared, the title had been changed to *Der Canadische Kolonist*, under which name it existed until July 1, 1906.

The initial number of the *Kolonist* appeared in the first week of January 1864. For nine years, Teuscher remained as publisher and editor of the *Kolonist*, relinquishing his duties in December 1872. His venture did not have the success that he had hoped for and disappointment pervades his farewell message found in number forty-eight of volume nine. He introduced J. H. Schmidt, the co-owner and editor of the *Chronicle* in Waterloo, with Michael Scherer, his partner, as the new owners of the *Kolonist*. Scherer had been the foreman in the *Bauernfreund* printing office in Preston in 1851, at the same time that Teuscher became editor of that weekly under Abraham A. Erb. Immediately prior to his entry into the partnership with Schmidt, Scherer was foreman in the *Chronicle* printing office in Waterloo.

Teuscher then gives the more cogent reasons for his withdrawal from the *Kolonist*. Among these he lists the evils of the credit system, financial losses he has suffered, insufficient public support, and the dissatisfaction of having spent twenty-one years of his life in journalism without ever realizing sufficient pecuniary rewards. He claims to have done his very best in the interests of the Germans in Canada. But the response from them has been poor as they are mainly farmers and artisans and have consequently little interest in newspapers and books. In addition the younger generation is being assimilated. Only in the Canadian Northwest may a more solid German settlement be hoped for with

a correspondingly better situation for German newspaper publishers. Circulation figures given in 1873, the year after Teuscher's retirement from the *Kolonist*, substantiate his assertion. According to these figures the *Kolonist* had an estimated circulation of 700.[12] In 1884, eleven years later, this number had barely increased beyond the 1000 mark.[13]

The *Kolonist* of Stratford was a very vigorous newspaper. Politics absorbed a major portion of the space devoted to news, although local items of a more intimate nature were not completely neglected. Humor, prose, poetry, as well as useful items of every variety, graced its columns. The editors often prodded their German readers to be more public-minded, and to throw themselves with greater energy into the life of the communities of which they were a part. They pointed out that no longer was it necessary for them to be the docile, servile subjects they had been before coming to Canada, where the freedom which had been denied them in their German fatherland, abounded.

In appearance the *Kolonist* followed the usual pattern of German newspapers in Ontario. By 1872, however, it had eight pages which were 20 inches high, 13 inches wide, with five columns of fairly fine print per page. Page size varied slightly from time to time. In 1872 the subscription price was two dollars per year. This was later dropped to $1.50 in advance.

J. H. Schmidt continued issuing the *Kolonist* until July 1, 1906, when, because of dwindling support, it was amalgamated with the *Berliner Journal*. By that time Schmidt was seventy-two years of age. In order to continue it would have been necessary for him to purchase a new typesetting machine. This would have been an expenditure which the financial prospects of the *Kolonist* would not have justified. In addition he found it difficult to secure the services of a German typesetter. Teuscher's gloomy prophecy of 1872 had evidently been fulfilled by 1906 in the Stratford area. Fusion and assimilation of the German element had proceeded to such an extent that a German newspaper found it difficult to maintain itself, and only the astute leadership of John Henry Schmidt kept the *Kolonist* from being submerged earlier.

Schmidt, the *Kolonist's* editor and publisher from 1877 to 1906, was a man of good background and training. Born in Lingelbach, in the Grand Duchy of Hessen in 1835, he was the son of Pastor Wilhelm Schmidt. His family migrated to Canada in 1836 and settled in New Hamburg. In 1854 John Henry Schmidt went to Delhi, Indiana; and in 1856 to Cincinnati to attend medical college. He returned to Canada in 1859 and became the principal of public schools in New Hamburg and Waterloo until 1869. With Thomas Hilliard he published an English newspaper, the Waterloo *Chronicle*, until 1872. He then purchased the *Kolonist* with Michael Scherer as partner. Schmidt was a Reformer in politics. He was on one occasion a candidate on the Reform platform for the legislature in Perth County but was unsuccessful. He was also for many years a member of the Stratford High School Board. From 1906 until his death in October, 1912, he operated a printing establishment in Stratford, where he was one of the town's most respected citizens.

Neujahrs-Glückwunsch
Der Träger des „Canadischen Kolonisten,"
an die geehrten Leser am 1. Januar 1875.
Wand-Kalender
für das Jahr 1875.
Die Träger des „Kolonisten."

Schmidt and Scherer remained partners on the *Kolonist* for five years, until 1877, when J. H. Schmidt acquired Scherer's portion of the venture.

After dissolving his partnership with Schmidt, Scherer started a German newspaper of his own in Stratford, the *Perth Volksfreund*, in July 1878. A special edition of the *Volksfreund*, with the title of the *Hamilton Anzeiger*, and edited by Geo. V. Hollen, was also published by Scherer for a short period in 1879, to serve the German readers in the Hamilton area. The *Volksfreund* was published for approximately two years in Stratford, then transferred to the village of Listowel in the first week of April 1880. The move was no doubt made in attempt to get away from the stronger and better established *Kolonist*. However, the flourishing period, for which this strongly Conservative organ hoped, did not materialize and in January 1883 the physical assets of the *Volksfreund* were sold by the sheriff. A German contemporary, whose political affiliations lay in the Liberal camp, noted that the policies of the Conservative party, the so-called National Policy, could not keep the *Perth Volksfreund* from bankruptcy. At its inception another and somewhat more friendly contemporary had expressed much more benevolent sentiments. This latter item appeared in the German section of the *Berlin Daily News* of July 15, 1878:

The Perth Volksfreund. On Saturday we had the pleasure of receiving the *Perth Volksfreund*, published in Stratford by M. Scherer. Our view about this paper can only be that it is a very satisfactory one. It contains an abundance of reading material, is well edited, has clear print, and in general leaves little to be desired. May Mr. Scherer have good success. We wish that his subscription list will increase rapidly.

The purchasers of the *Volksfreund's* equipment immediately set about to publish a new *Listowel Volksfreund* under the editorship of Dr. Alois Sommer, a Lutheran minister of that village. This arrangement lasted for about six months at which time Sommer resigned his position. The *Volksfreund* then passed permanently out of existence. The *Ontario Glocke* in Walkerton was given its subscription list and a correspondent, John B. Dinkel, became a regular reporter to the *Glocke* from Listowel. Michael Scherer later became press foreman on the *Berlin News*, subsequently press foreman on the *Deutsche Zeitung* of Berlin and, for a short time, its editor. He died in Berlin on December 21, 1902, at the age of sixty-five years.

The village of Preston, which had been the point of origin of several German weekly newspapers, all of which had only brief periods of existence in that village before either suspending publication or moving to other locations, became the scene of a new *Beobachter*, published by Wilhelm Schlüter, from approximately 1856 to 1867.

Schlüter was born at Köthen in the Duchy of Anhalt, Germany, on November 28, 1800. He had studied philology at Halle before migrating to the United States in 1843. In 1845 he founded the *New Yorker Demokrat* with Anthony Dugro as partner. This paper began as a weekly but was changed into a daily in 1846. Schlüter also organized the first building society in New York in 1854. In 1855 he printed Gustav Struve's *Weltge-*

schichte, a history of the world in nine volumes written from a democratic point of view.

In 1856 Schlüter left New York and went to Toronto, Canada. Here he founded *Der Beobachter,* of which he was editor, proprietor and publisher. It was a weekly with an annual subscription price of two dollars. Toronto soon proved to be an unfavorable location for a German newspaper; consequently *Der Beobachter* was transferred to Preston where, as noted above, it continued to appear for a period of about ten years. A short time after suspension of publication the physical equipment of *Der Beobachter* was sold to Victor Lang and Christian Heise. Schlüter, who died on January 2, 1882, remained in Preston as a printer after the *Beobachter* ceased publication.

Until 1868 German newspapers had been established mainly in Waterloo County; one, *Der Canadische Kolonist,* of Stratford, in the adjoining county of Perth, began its existence four years earlier, in 1864. In December 1868 the geographical limits within which German newspapers appeared were further enlarged by the appearance of a German weekly in Grey County on Georgian Bay. Since its location was in Neustadt on the Saugeen River, it was appropriately named *Der Wächter am Saugeen.* It was published by the partnership of Victor Lang and Christian Heise, and its first number appeared on December 18, 1868. The presses, type, and other printing equipment, as has been noted above, had been purchased from Wilhelm Schlüter, formerly publisher and editor of the *Beobachter* in Preston. At its inception, the subscription price was $ 1.50 in advance, or $ 2.00 if paid later. In politics the *Wächter* proposed to steer a strictly neutral course.

The partnership of Lang and Heise lasted about two and a half years, when Lang became the sole owner of the *Wächter.* For a short period the paper suspended publication, but by October 1872 it resumed its appearance. In May 1876 the *Wächter* again changed hands. It was bought by John and A. A. Klein who ran it until 1881. In 1879 its name was changed to the *Canada National-Zeitung,* and its size was increased. At the same time the annual subscription price was reduced to $1.25 per year. Both measures — changing of the name and the reduction in subscription price — were evidently designed to revivify the venture. A fire in 1882, however, destroyed the Klein home as well as the printing office and no attempt was made to revive the *National-Zeitung.*

Of the two founders of the *Wächter,* Victor Lang was the better known in his community. Born at Waibstadt, Grand Duchy of Baden, he had come to Canada in 1847. From 1853 to 1855 he was an apprentice with Martin Rudolph in New Hamburg. He then went for a short time to Neustadt as an elementary school teacher, returning, however, again to the printing business in Waterloo County. In 1863 he settled permanently in Neustadt, where he became the co-founder of the *Wächter,* which he edited until 1876. In addition he served as reeve of Normanby Township for twelve years, during one of which he was warden of

Grey County. He died at the age of fifty-two years in Neustadt in April 1894.

Der Wächter am Saugeen was a weekly of four pages which were 20 inches high and 13 inches wide. By 1873 it boasted a circulation of 720.[14] Four years later it claimed a circulation of only 700. It was now published by John Klein and Son, with the former as its editor. That it did not lack confidence in its own importance may be gathered from what it said about itself in an American publication: "... *Der Wächter am Saugeen* is a

large and influential German newspaper, devoted to advocacy of the interests and views of Canadian Germans, without party consideration. It circulates through the German counties of Grey, Bruce, Wellington, Waterloo, Huron, and Welland, and is the best medium for reaching the intelligent Germans of this portion of the Dominion . . .".[15]

Another American source gives it an estimated circulation of only 500 one year previously, in 1876.[16]

John Klein, its last editor, was born in Alsace, and came to Canada in 1833 at the age of eight years. He entered the teaching profession in Waterloo County, later proceeding to Walkerton, where he founded *Die Glocke* in 1869, of which he was editor, proprietor and printer. After the sale of this newspaper to Dr. Aaron Eby and John A. Rittinger in December 1875, he purchased, as noted above, the *Wächter* in Neustadt from Victor Lang in 1876. In addition to his editorial duties he was also a notary and a commissioner in Queen's Bench in Walkerton. The year following the destruction of his home and printing establishment in Neustadt, he returned to Walkerton, where he lived until his death in November 1918.

Elmira, in Waterloo County, and Walkerton, in Bruce County, became the scenes of the establishment of German newspapers in the beginning of the year 1870. Of the two, the *Elmira Anzeiger* was the first to appear. Its initial number was printed in the second week of January 1870. It was sponsored by the firm of Philip Pfaff and David Wittig. It was a neatly printed weekly of four pages with twenty-eight columns, with a subscription price of $1.50 in advance, or $1.75 after three months. After a month the two partners abandoned the venture and for several weeks the *Anzeiger* did not appear. By the end of February 1870, however, the Delion brothers, Frederick and William, purchased the business from the original owners and the newspaper appeared regularly again every Thursday. For thirteen years, until the end of 1882, the Delions continued to publish the *Anzeiger*. Support, both in advertising and in subscriptions, however, dropped off to such an extent that a continuation of the *Anzeiger* was no longer a practical possibility. Its printing equipment and other assets were sold and an English newspaper, the *Elmira Advertiser*, was issued from its press. There is only meagre information to be obtained regarding the circulation of the *Anzeiger*. An American source gives it an estimated 300 subscribers in 1876. In a local publication the *Anzeiger* said of itself:

The *Anzeiger* has a very large circulation in North Waterloo among the business men and farming community, which renders it an excellent medium for advertising. It contains the latest foreign and local news up to date of publication.[17]

The *Anzeiger* was still listed by Heinrich Lemcke in *Canada, das Land und seine Leute* in 1887, five years after it had ceased appearing.[18]

The Walkerton German newspaper founded in the same year as the *Anzeiger* was of a much hardier variety than its Elmira contemporary, and lasted over thirty years. Named the *Walkerton Glocke*, its initial number appeared in the first week of February 1870 with an annual subscription price of $1.50. At the outset it supported the Liberal party. Its founder, who was also its owner, editor, and printer, was John Klein, later associated with *Der Wächter am Saugeen*. He retained the *Glocke* in his possession until December 1875 when, as mentioned above, it passed into the hands of Dr. Aaron Eby and John A. Rittinger, the latter the son of Friedrich Rittinger of the *Berliner Journal*. Rittinger had learned the printing trade in the office of the *Journal*, and also had had further experience in the printing trade in Toronto, Buffalo, and Chicago before he joined Dr. Eby on the *Glocke*. Dr. Eby was Canadian-born of Pennsylvania German descent and came from the same stock as the other Ebys whose names are associated with various German newspapers in Ontario. He was one of the few members of the Pennsylvania German group who was sufficiently German in his outlook to satisfy the foreign-born Germans.

The partnership of Eby and Rittinger lasted until June 1878, when it was dissolved, and John A. Rittinger became the sole owner and editor of the *Glocke* during the remainder of its life. After the dissolution of the partnership Eby printed a small sheet in German in Walkerton, called *Die Post*. It appeared in the interests of the Reform party, but it never developed into a full-fledged competitor of the *Glocke*, and was discontinued in January 1879.

In 1882 the *Walkerton Glocke* was renamed *Die Ontario Glocke*, and enlarged from a four to an eight-page weekly. As an eight-page paper its subscription price remained at $1.50 if paid in advance, or $2.00 if paid later. It was 21 inches high, 15 inches wide, with six columns per page. The *Glocke* prided itself on the amount of reading material it contained, and said so in its own columns.

In 1873 an American publication gave the *Glocke* an estimated circulation of 520.[19] At this time it still was a paper of four pages and measured 20 inches high and 13 wide. Eleven years later, in 1884, a Canadian source gave it a subscription list of close to 2000.[20] These estimates cannot be accepted as even remotely accurate, since, according to circulation figures printed in the *Glocke* of December 19, 1883, it stated that its subscription list had risen from 350 in 1878 to between 1300 and 1400 in 1883. This was indeed a phenomenal growth and even if not as spectacular as the above estimate of 1884, it must, in part at least, be attributed to the ability and popularity of its publisher and editor, John A. Rittinger. A good businessman, he owned his printing establishment as a debt-free enterprise by 1891. And this was accomplished in spite of the fact that he had acquired a new steam press in 1883 at a cost of approximately $1600. It is a fairly safe guess to say that he knew personally every subscriber to his weekly, by whom as well as by others he was affectionately known as the "*Glockemann*".

The *Glocke* carried on until 1904 when, on July 1 of that year, it was amalgamated with the *Berliner Journal*. John A. Rittinger, after publishing the *Glocke* in Walkerton for twenty-six years, now moved to Berlin and became the responsible editor of the new *Journal-Glocke*. This move was considered necessary to maintain the strength of the German newspaper press, and to assure the employment of the most modern equipment and printing techniques. Henceforth the contents of the two papers were the same, the only distinguishing mark being in the different mastheads. Although twelve instead of eight pages constituted each weekly issue, the price was not advanced.

In appearance and general arrangement the *Glocke* resembled its Ontario German contemporaries. Professional notices and foreign news usually occupied the first page; then followed a *feuilleton*, humor, advertisements, local, Canadian and United States events, poetry, and articles of general interest. A good balance between the various features was constantly maintained. The printing was always excellent and the reading of proofs done with meticulous care. As time went on many items in Pennsylvania or local German dialect began to make their appearance. These items were most frequently in the form of articles or correspondence and appeared over the names of various characters, in every case fictitious. Among them are *Pid Schnitzmacher, Missgawels Hanjerk, Hickory Jackson, Sam Quetschekern, D'r Hansjörg, Joe Klotzkopp,* and *Särah Klotzkopp*, Joe's wife. Of these, the letters from *Joe Klotzkopp* became a popular feature of the *Glocke* and later, after amalgamation, of the *Berliner Journal*, and of other German papers which combined with it. The first *Joe Klotzkopp* letter seems to have appeared in the *Glocke* on January 22, 1890. Further letters emanating from him were published at intervals during that year until November. In response to subscriber demand they were resumed the following and subsequent years. The readers of the *Glocke* looked upon *Joe Klotzkopp* as a necessary adjunct to their reading pleasure, and even went so far as to memorize and quote passages from him especially noted for their humorous quality, or those which contained kernels of good homespun philosophy. So intent were the readers on following *Joe Klotzkopp* that the editor of the *Glocke*, who, as we later discover, was the author of the letters, found it necessary to apprise the public from time to time as to the whereabouts and the plans of its popular idol. *Joe Klotzkopp*, his doings and sayings, as well as those of his wife *Särah*, became topics of conversation wherever the *Glocke*, and later, after the period of amalgamation, the *Berliner Journal* and the variously captioned members of its family were read. Many readers, whose knowledge of a good German standard had considerably deteriorated, were attracted by the dialect which *Joe Klotzkopp* and others of his breed employed, and were retained as subscribers of the German newspapers by such devices.

The reason for the spread of the Pennsylvania-German dialect throughout the German-speaking areas in Ontario stemmed from the fact that the German citadel in Ontario, Waterloo County, had originally been peopled with settlers from Pennsylvania. This county became, as time went on, more or less the processing point of German immigrants into south-western Ontario. It was because of this fact that the Pennsylvania-German dialect became the predominant oral vehicle of all the Germans in Ontario, irrespective of their point of origin. Only the press and, to some extent, the pulpit contrived to hold themselves aloof from this all-pervading dialect. But the press, then as now, was sensitive to public opinion, and in its urge to satisfy all segments of its clientèle, compromised by providing Pennsylvania-German material, construing it, however, as the language of humor, in contrast to factual reporting, which was done in the best standard of German of which the editors were capable. The maintenance of a good standard, in the absence of corrective influences, was no mean task. Frequent references are to be found in newspapers in the fatherland, calling attention to the deterioration of both word and idiom in the Ontario German newspapers. This deterioration was inevitable, as few educated German journalists ever set foot on Canadian soil, and the few who did soon travelled south of the border, where the rewards were greater than in Canada.

With few exceptions the Pennsylvania-German material appearing in the Ontario German newspapers originated in the United States. The *Briefe vun Joe Klotzkopp* provide one of the most notable exceptions. Had John A. Rittinger written in English, he would be counted among the great humorists of this country. His work is in the tradition of Thomas Chandler Haliburton and Stephen Leacock. Even in translation the subtle sallies are not lost. Rittinger was against prohibition and in a letter of December 13, 1893, he gave vent to his feelings as follows:

At the moment everyone is talking about prohibition. My neighbor says that if the majority votes for it, we shall certainly get prohibition. "Yes," I said, "and the cows will fly to pasture next spring, if they sprout wings." I am not afraid of the temperance people; I know them too well. Their bite is not half so bad as their bark. They remind me frequently of the boy who was asked by someone if his father were a Christian. "Yes," he answered, "but he does not work very hard at it."

A short while ago I was at a temperance meeting. The lecturer lambasted the use of alcohol and opined: "The quantity of intoxicating liquor consumed in this country makes me dizzy." A man at the back of the hall, who tried his best to keep himself upright by clinging to the plaster on the wall, suddenly shouted: "me too.".[21]

There was no dearth of prose and poetic material in the *Glocke*. The continued story was a regular feature and each issue contained a generous portion of the particular novel or short story then appearing. Seven and more columns in an individual number was the usual share, and a fairly large-sized novel would appear in the course of a few months. The prose fiction, as was usual in the German newspapers, was the work of contemporary authors, many of whom achieved only passing significance. A random selection of prose authors and their works represented in the offerings of the *Glocke* from 1883 to 1893 reveals the following: Marie Stielow with *Edeltanne*, Euphemia Gräfin

Ballestrem with *Glück und Leid*, Berthold Auerbach with *Der Tolpatsch*, Karl Hoffmann with *Die Circuskönigin*, L. Reynolds with *Eine Amerikanische Mutter oder Glanz und Elend in New York* (ran from October 8, 1884 to March 18, 1885), Friedrich Gerstäcker with *Der Kunstreiter* and *Der Wilddieb*, Otto Ruppius (the well-known Forty-Eighter) with *Der Prairie-Teufel*, Friedrich Spielhagen with *Hans und Grete*, Hermine Frankenstein with *Hütte und Palast*, Detlev Freiherr von Liliencron with *Umzingelt*, Gräfin M. Keyserling with *Brandtmann's Tochter*, Ludwig Ganghofer with *Der Besondere*, Rheinhold Ortmann with *Der Bankdirektor*, Ludwig Habicht with *Auf der Grenzwacht*, James Fenimore Cooper with *Der Spion* (a translation), and Woldemar Urban with *Vor Hundert Jahren*. In addition there was a considerable bulk of anonymous prose fiction during the same period.

The literary quality of the prose was, on the whole, better than that of the poetry. Serious poetry by the best authors is conspicuously scarce in relation to the total quantity of verse contained in the *Glocke*. The lighter and more humorous effusions of minor poetizers seemed to have had wide popularity with the readers. A selection, again from the ten-year period 1883-1893, shows the following anonymous poems: *Großmutter, Sommernacht, Petrus und das Hufeisen, Der Durst der Schwaben* (dialect), *Liebe zur deutschen Heimath, Die Macht der Gewohnheit, Bleibet Deutsch, Der todte Soldat, Die deutsche Sprache, Der Muckelhans von Schilda, Hochsommer, Ein Gruß an die Deutschen in Nord-Amerika*, and *Das Menschenherz*. The more reputable contemporary German poets are, however, not completely neglected. They are represented in the above period by Rudolf Baumbach with *Liebchen*, Emanuel Geibel with *Der Goldgräber*, Friedrich Bodenstedt with *Herbstgefühle*, Franz X. Seidel with *Abendglocke*, Karl Gerok with *Vor Weihnachten*, Ferdinand Freiligrath with *Der Liebe Dauer*, Johannes Trojan with *Wo kommt das Brod her?*, Emil Gött with *Sprüchworte* and *Stichworte*, and Kaiser Wilhelm I. (evidently a gesture toward the aging German Emperor who was approaching the end of his long reign) with *Der Oberrhein*. Of particular delight to the readers seem to have been long rhymes on questions of the day or other burning topics which usually appeared under the *noms de plume* of either *Jeremias Federmann* or *Glycerinus Bombenmeyer*. Again in the 1883 to 1893 period we find under this heading the following: *Jeremias Federmann über die Schwiegermütter, Jeremias Federmann über das Sauerkraut* and *Glycerinus Bombenmeyer über den Limburger*.

From the above it becomes evident that the *Glocke* spared no effort to present something for everyone in the way of reading material. There was at all times a good selection of short articles on a multiplicity of subjects ranging from philosophy and science, through politics, the useful arts as well as an occasional sally into the area of the bizarre and the scandalous for those who relished such items. It must be stated, however, that the *Glocke* appealed to the best instincts of the community and never stooped to the sensational or emotional in order to curry popularity.

The *Glocke* was very active politically. It supported the Conservative party after Rittinger became its sole owner and editor, although it did not do so slavishly. It was sufficiently independent to disagree, particularly when it felt that its interests or those of the German population were being threatened by the policies of that party. It clashed particularly with the stand taken by the Conservatives in regard to German language instruction in the schools of Ontario, and expressed itself vigorously on this question. It carried on, as may be expected, a bold campaign in support of German language teaching in the elementary and secondary schools in German communities, and was emphatic in denying that the study of the German language militated against a fervent patriotism on the part of German-Canadians.[22] At the same time it made strenuous efforts to initiate the Germans who were already here, and those who were arriving, into the political ways of Canada. It hailed, in common with most of the German newspapers of Ontario, the increasing power and prestige of the unified Germany, but it was not blind to the political advantages enjoyed by Canadians in contrast to the Germans. Bismarck was lauded because of his successful policies, but the lack of freedom of the press in Germany was execrated. Particularly did it express concern at the many court actions taken in the fatherland against newspaper editors for *lèse majesté*. It shared the general opinion of the German newspapers in Ontario that only a free press could serve the best interests of a land whose governmental policy aimed at securing the best possible conditions for the greatest number.

Queen Victoria was regarded with a feeling of sentimental attachment. Her association by marriage with various German royal households, and her ability to speak and write German fluently evoked a sympathetic response from the *Glocke*, and indeed from Ontario German newspapers generally. This loyalty to the Queen was reflected in poems and articles and inspired loyalty to Canada. Her Majesty's representatives never failed to take notice of her loyal subjects of German origin in the Ontario communities.

The *Glocke* regularly featured an editorial column. The dominant items in this column were political. Domestic issues were discussed with conviction and acumen. It favored, as already noted, the policies of the Conservative party, including the high tariff plank of that party, generally known as the National Policy. Nativism in any guise was combatted and so was prohibition. Individual freedom was espoused and religious controversy avoided.

The *Glocke* was a strong supporter of German drama and German music. It deplored the fact that its immediate area was not adapted to the formation of German societies to carry on these cultural activities. The sections of Bruce and Grey counties which it served were largely agricultural, and the villages and towns in them did not have a sufficient concentration of German population to make a *Turnverein* or similar organization possible, although the *Glocke* advocated the formation of a general organization comprehending the Germans in the counties of Grey and Bruce in 1893. In its news items it always furnished details about the cultural activities of German groups everywhere in Canada.

A much enhanced quantity of local news began to appear in the columns of the *Glocke* in the 1890's. Local correspondents were employed in the various German communities. These men also served as its representatives und agents. They reported intimate items from Mildmay, Hanover, Formosa, Chepstow, Elmwood, Ayton and Carlsruhe. This new feature impinged on the space formerly allotted to foreign news which, in consequence, was reduced in quantity. Almost simultaneous with this innovation was another: the inclusion of local news from the German areas in Europe. Very frequently these columns contained quite intimate happenings which had no wider significance than to the relatives and friends of those concerned. They might be construed as small voices from the homeland designed to soothe nostalgic feelings in those who had wandered so far from it.

The *Glocke* was usually on friendly terms with most of its German contemporaries, but there were exceptions. Sometimes tempers were only temporarily ruffled because of some disagreement on a political matter, then again lack of proper credit for a quotation may have evoked a sharp broadside, or a feud was carried on more or less acrimoniously because of a basic difference in viewpoint, which may or may not have involved personalities. Rittinger could frame an acrid retort if the occasion warranted it and sometimes did so. In 1891 an extended feud was carried on with the newly-established *Deutsche Zeitung* of Berlin. The contentious subject was mainly orthography and the German style of the new paper and was partly inspired, no doubt, by the attempt on the part of the new weekly to lure away subscribers from the *Glocke,* as well as in retaliation for a slander suit involving a claim for five thousand dollars which Pastor R. von Pirch, the prime personality in the new *Deutsche Zeitung,* had preferred against John A. Rittinger in 1885. Pirch had won a technical victory in this clash by being awarded damages of one dollar by the court. The *Deutsche Zeitung* was never viewed with a tolerant eye during the whole period of its existence by the *Glocke.*

The *Ontario Glocke* of Walkerton was one of the five major German newspapers of Ontario. Its excellence must in large measure be attributed to its capable editor and publisher, John A. Rittinger, who for twenty-six years bore the burden of its editorial and publishing duties. His abilities clearly manifest themselves in his product; abilities which made him the logical choice as responsible editor of the new and enlarged *Berliner Journal* and *Glocke* after amalgamation of these two in 1904. In this period, when assimilation and fusion of the German minority with the English-speaking majority had progressed considerably, J. A. Rittinger was still able to edit a German newspaper which maintained its appeal, even among those of the German community who no longer spoke German fluently, and among whom many were beginning to read it with some difficulty. His death on July 29, 1915, removed him at a time

Neujahrs - Gruß

1873.

Den Lesern der Canadischen Volkszeitung

gewidmet.

Hamilton, den 1. Januar 1873.

Viel Glück zum neuen Jahre! erschallt heut' unser Ruf;
Das alte ist vergangen, das Lust und Leid uns schuf.
Es mög' das neue bringen der Freuden große Zahl,
Und Segen und Gedeihen den Menschen allzumal.

Wem Wunden es geschlagen, das hingeschwund'ne Jahr,
Wem Trauer es bereitet und Sorgen und Gefahr,
Ihm mög' das neue bringen des Glückes volle Hand,
Den Kranken und dem Siechen Ergebung und Geduld.

Den Reichen warme Herzen, zu lindern andrer Noth,
Den Armen reiche Spenden für's liebe tägliche Brod;
Dem Händler gute Geschäfte, dem Arbeiter reichlichen Lohn,
Den Bauern volle Scheunen, dem Freund L. L.—einen Sohn.

Den Stadtvätern helle Köpfe, den Gesetzgebern viel Verstand,
Den Wassersimpeln Wasser, die Fässer voll zum Rand.
Uns Andern aber verschone, du liebes neues Jahr
Mit Temperenzgesetzen und sonstiger Muckerplag'.

Und willst Du, neugebor'nes, [illegible] Jahr,
Uns ganz besonders erfreuen, so mache die blos gar:
Daß uns're Polizisten mehr nach den Dieben seh'n,
Statt daß sie Samstag Abends so viel um die Wirthshäuser
geh'n.

Die Wirthe sind auch Menschen, die leben wollen, auch, seht:
Man trinkt auch wohl einen Schoppen am Sonntag in der
Früh,
Ein Schoppen in allen Ehren, das mag doch wohl angehn,
Drum laß keinen Polizisten die Hinterthüren sehn.

Was sollen wir ferner noch wünschen? Den Völkern Frieden
und Ruh,
Dem lieben deutschen Reiche das beste Gedeihen dazu;
Dem Bismarck langes Leben und immer frischen Muth,
Denn wenn der dort sollte fehlen, geht's sicher niemals gut.

Dem Franzmann Lösung der Wirren, die wieder das Land be-
drohn
Im Kampfe der Parteien, im Ringen um den Thron.
Unsern Nachbarn, den Herrn Yankees, ein wenig Bescheidenheit,
Wenn sich's um Canada handelt, um unser Land und Leut'.

Dem Deutschen Graf nicht wieder, kein zweites Schiedsgericht;
Dem Spanier Muth und Einsicht, dann fällt die Sklaverei nicht.
Dem Papste endlich Frieden, dem Italiener sein einig Reich,
Und recht viel baare Münze dem armen Oesterreich.

Zum Schlusse nun noch wünschen wir uns selbst ein gutes Jahr,
Die Gunst von allen Deutschen, denn so wird es doch klar:
Wenn Jeder sich abonnirt und pünktlich dann auch „blecht,"
Dann wird die „Volks-Zeitung" auch allem Volk gerecht.

of supreme crisis in the history of German journalism in Ontario. It was almost as if his passing were a portent of that day, only slightly more than three years later, when German newspapers in Canada were to be banned by government decree. Fate spared him the trials and disappointments of the most critical years of the first World War, and called him away just before the edifice, which he had so painstakingly helped to construct, toppled into ruin.

For a very short period in the 1870's a German weekly was published at the hamlet of Wartburg, not far from Mitchell, Ontario. Little information is available about this weekly and there are no extant files. It is mentioned in *Deutsch-Amerikanisches Conversations-Lexicon*, edited by Alexander J. Schem, as having been in existence in 1871 [23], but it must have disappeared before 1873 as he no longer included it in a list of Canadian German newspapers given in that year. [24] Its German journalistic rivals in Western Ontario seem to have regarded it as only of passing significance. The *Berliner Journal*, which never failed to record the appearance, as well as the demise, of German newspapers in this area, makes no mention whatever of *Die Wespe*.

In April 1871 a German monthly journal began to make its appearance in London, Ontario. It was named *Der Deutsche in Canada* and was published and edited by Charles Mack, whose real name, however, was Conrad Marxhausen. He went under both the names of Charles Mack as well as Charles Marxhausen while he resided in London, no doubt chiefly because of the almost solid English character of that city's population. He was a printer by profession and served as the foreman of the book and job printing department of the London *Advertiser*. He also carried a stock of German books which, prior to his embarking on the publication of *Der Deutsche in Canada*, he advertised in the *Berliner Journal*.

London was not a favorable location for a German newspaper and, after approximately a year, Marxhausen moved to Hamilton, Ontario, where, in November 1872 he began publishing a German weekly, the *Canadische Volkszeitung*. He also continued *Der Deutsche in Canada* as a monthly in Hamilton at the same time.

The weekly *Canadische Volkszeitung* had four pages which measured 12 inches wide and 18 inches high, with a subscription price of two dollars per annum. An American newspaper directory gives it an estimated circulation of 800 in 1873. [25]

The monthly *Der Deutsche in Canada* comprised twenty-four pages, 9 inches wide and 12 inches tall, also with a subscription price of two dollars per year. The above-mentioned newspaper directory gives it an estimated circulation of 1200 in 1873.

It is quite evident that these estimates were considerably exaggerated, and that Marxhausen hoped through this method to create the illusion of prosperity in order to arouse confidence among the subscribers as well as among the advertisers in his venture.

Until April 1875 both papers appeared in Hamilton, when, with very little notice, they suspended publication. In the following month, *Der Deutsche in Canada*, printed partly in Latin and partly in German type, made its reappearance in London. The middle of July 1875 also witnessed the rebirth of the *Canadische Volkszeitung* in London. The beginning of January 1876, however, marked the end of both these newspapers, and Marxhausen moved to Detroit. He died at East Saginaw, Michigan, on September 24, 1882, at the age of fifty-one years. Born in 1831 at Kassel, Hesse, Germany, he had migrated to the United States in 1851. Together with his brother, August Marxhausen, he had assisted in the founding of the *Michigan Journal* at Detroit, and later in the same city of the *Sonntagszeitung*.

Marxhausen's career in Canada was, in addition to the fluctuating fortunes in his journalistic ventures, not altogether uneventful in other respects. An item in the *Canadisches Volksblatt* of September 6, 1871, taken from the *Michigan Volksblatt* brought the following:

Conrad Marxhausen, the former publisher of the *Michigan Journal*, about whose "note operations" and other stratagems and sharp practices we brought a rather complete report a little over a year ago, is here since yesterday evening, but not in a first-class hotel, but in the lock-up. A local bank, with which he had done some "note business" in the name of Mr. B. Stroh (but without the latter's knowledge) wanted to be reimbursed for the Marxhausian music. Mr. Stroh "settled," as we have heard, a part of the claims, but then to throw away another 1200 to 1500 dollars without getting anything in return, was too much even for a man as rich as Mr. Stroh. The bank accordingly issued a warrant for the arrest of the note manufacturer, C. Marxhausen, on Monday. Yesterday detective Stadler brought him over safe and sound from Canada. What the bank actually wishes to do with him is not yet certain. However, some people conjecture that it intends to enter him as Republican candidate for the position of city treasurer, while others think that Mr. Conrad Marxhausen should be employed as a composer because he is so adept in the manufacturing of "notes". The musicians protest against this suggestion because his notes are all false.

One week later, on September 13, 1871, the London *Advertiser* was quoted, again in the *Volksblatt*, to the effect that Chas. Mack had been honorably acquitted on the above charge. It noted that henceforth he would go under his German name of Conrad Marxhausen. Our comment must be that he evidently escaped rather easily from what looked like a nasty situation.

In 1872 the publishers of the German newspapers in Ontario decided to form a press association to further their interests, and to have an organization which could speak in the name of the whole group. The first meeting of the *Deutsch-Canadischer Pressverein* (German-Canadian Press Association), as it called itself, was held at Waterloo on July 2, 1872. The following newspapers were represented: the *Kolonist* by Jakob Teuscher, *Der Deutsche in Canada* by Conrad Marxhausen, the *Bauernfreund* by Joachim Kalbfleisch, the *Anzeiger* by Frederick Delion, the *Wächter* by Victor Lang, and the *Journal* by John Motz. This meeting was mainly exploratory and no business was transacted. It was decided to hold an organizational meeting in Berlin on September 5, 1872. On that occasion the above newspapers were represented with the exception of the *Elmira Anzeiger*, but this loss was made up by the presence of Otto Pressprich of the *Volksblatt*. The election of officers resulted in John Motz becoming president, Otto Pressprich secretary, and Victor Lang, treasurer, of the association. Two items of business were discussed and the following resolutions were drawn up: (1) That the *Pressverein* petition the Ontario

Legislature to put the German-English schools in Ontario on the same basis as the English schools; (2) That the *Pressverein* petition the Executive, the Senate, and the House of Commons of the Dominion of Canada to prevail on the British Government to make the status of a British subject by naturalization equal to that of a British subject by birth.

There is no report in any of the German newspapers as to the reception of and response to the above resolutions. The first resolution was a favorite theme of the newspapers at all times, and continued to be so until the outbreak of the first World War. German schools and German in the English public schools were constantly advocated also by other German groups and individuals. The *Evangelische Gemeinschaft* (Evangelical Church) petitioned the Ontario government in 1873 to appoint German professors at the Normal Schools in Ontario, and also to provide German school inspectors for the German schools in the province. This church body contended that English and German speaking teachers were needed for the German areas. The second resolution submitted at the September meeting of the *Pressverein* has remained a topic of interest to immigrants right up to our own time. Many newcomers to Canada feel that they cannot rise beyond the status of a second-class citizen, even though naturalized and willing to conform to the manners and mores of the new land.

The meeting of the *Pressverein* of September 5, 1872, was adjourned to meet again on July 1, 1873, in Neustadt, but there is no report in any of the German newspapers of this proposed meeting being held. It must be assumed that for some reason or other it was not, and that no further attempt was made to keep the organization alive.

On Saturday, February 9, 1878, the first English daily newspaper in Berlin, the *Berlin Daily News*, made its appearance under the editorship of P. E. W. Moyer. It was a four-page paper, 15 inches wide and 19 1/2 inches high, with three solid pages in English and a portion of page four in German. This German page contained local news items, foreign and Canadian political happenings, humor, poetry and miscellaneous prose material. In the beginning about half of the page was given over to advertisements in English. The serial story was represented with *Der Mops* by Stanislaus Graf Grabowski, which ran from March 29 to April 18, 1878. During the same period there also appeared serially *Gefährliche Theatermomente* by Leopold von Sacher-Masoch (the Austrian novelist from whose name the term "masochism" is derived), *Eine Tyroler Geschichte* by Heinrich Laube, as well as a number of anoymous stories and works of minor writers.

The poetry was mainly anonymous and of mediocre quality. The titles, such as *Der Dollar unserer Väter, Sauerkraut Lied, Rumpelmeiers Lösung der socialen Frage, Heiraths-Antrag, Lebensregel*, and *Herbst Gruß*, clearly indicate its lowly inspiration.

As time went on, the quantity of German material in the *News* decreased and on October 16, 1878, the section was competely omitted. No explanation was given for this sudden move. The editor of the section had on a number of occasions pleaded with the Germans to retain a speaking and reading knowledge of their language. He also made concessions to the local dialect by including a number of dialect letters in the German columns. Among these were *Brief vun Mary Beißzang, Brief vun Blockstädtel,* and *Die Schoofbock-Pärthie* by Hornessel.

The German section, in harmony with the political orientation of the *News,* gave strong support to the Conservative party. Nearly the whole section during the month of August, 1878, was devoted to campaign material for the Conservative side in the forthcoming election.

Almost simultaneously with the *Berlin Daily News,* there appeared in Berlin a German newspaper published also by P. E. W. Moyer under the title of *Das Wochenblatt.* It was evidently intended that this weekly should be a companion to the *Daily News* and draw the German newspaper reading public likewise into the Moyer orbit. The subscription price of *Das Wochenblatt* was one dollar per annum in advance. It had four large-sized pages measuring 26 3/4 inches high and 20 1/2 inches wide. The first number, which appeared on February 19, 1878, came exactly ten days after the first number of the *Daily News.*

Das Wochenblatt, like the *Daily News,* supported the Conservative party and gave much space to news about that party. It differed little from the other German weeklies of the time, except that its advertising material was mainly in English. In addition it also published English notices, poetry, articles, and news items. It ran for only a few weeks and then disappeared.

In the village of Ayton, in Grey County, a German newspaper was brought into existence in January 1882. It was a weekly of four pages, 28 1/2 inches high and 20 1/2 inches wide. Its name was *Die Aytoner Fama* with Gottfried Voigt as editor. Voigt called himself an educated Prussian village scholar. The *Fama* found little favor with its German contemporaries and had great difficulty in maintaining itself. It was often at odds with its more firmly established neighbor, the *Ontario Glocke* of Walkerton, whose editor on occasion felt himself obliged to instruct Voigt on the proper use of the German language.

In November 1890 the *Fama* moved from Ayton to Neustadt and changed its name to *Der Canadische Volksfreund.* In January 1892 the paper was purchased by H. J. Schwartz, with Gottfried Voigt remaining as editor. In May of 1892, however, Voigt decided to suspend publication of the *Volksfreund.* He left Ayton in the same month for New York, from which port he sailed for Germany, where he intended to retire.

For a period of approximately fifteen months, a German newspaper was published in the Niagara Peninsula at Welland, Ontario. It was called the *Welland Deutscher Telegraph* and was published by the *Welland Verlags-Anstalt.* The first number of this weekly appeared in March 1885, the last in the beginning of June 1886. It seems that the *Deutscher Telegraph* was merely a translation of the weekly edition of the English *Welland Telegraph* which was owned by the partnership of Sawle and Snarrt at the time. Snarrt soon withdrew from the company as he could not raise sufficient money to pay for his share of the stock and Sawle carried on alone. The editor of the *Deutscher Telegraph* was W. H. House, who remained with the English *Telegraph* for several years after his German edition had failed. He subsequently took a position with the Canadian customs offices at Fort Erie and Niagara Falls.

The *Deutscher Telegraph* attracted some notice on the part of its German contemporaries when it first appeared. Its disappearance, however, in 1886, attracted even more attention in contemporary German newspaper circles. The failure of a competitor was frequently given much more space by the more persistent German weeklies than the appearance of a new one. The frantic struggle for self-preservation revealed itself in the almost malicious satisfaction with which rival editors viewed the eventual demise of a competitor. In 1888, Wilhelm Joest, in *Die außereuropäische deutsche Presse* (The German Press outside Europe), still listed the *Telegraph* as an active newspaper, although by that time it had already slumbered for two years.[26]

The *Welland Deutscher Telegraph* was an attempt made locally to provide a German newspaper for the German-speaking residents of the Niagara Peninsula. Its brief existence must be ascribed to lack of support.

The history of the early German weeklies outside of Waterloo County, and more specifically its chief town, Berlin, is with very few exceptions a story of unfulfilled hopes. Often the newspaper was made possible largely by the job printing that was done in the same office. But in Berlin certain individuals or the supporters of certain interests sometimes entered the field to promote an enthusiasm or to articulate the ideas of the group that sponsored them. Such a weekly was the *Freie Presse*, which made its initial appearance in Berlin on August 6, 1886. Its avowed aim was to supplant all other German weekly newspapers published in Ontario. According to its prospectus it was presenting itself in answer to a long-felt demand for a new German paper in the heart of the German community. The *Freie Presse* was to be an ardent supporter of the Conservative party. Its subscription price was $ 1.50 per year, and its publishers were at the outset the firm of Hett and Buchhaupt. It was an eight-page paper with six columns per page and was 21 inches high and 14 1/2 inches wide. The first page was given over completely to a weekly review of foreign and American news. A prose page followed with the usual continued story as the main feature. Then followed miscellaneous items, the editorial page, local notes, articles on many subjects, and advertising copy. At the beginning the ratio of advertising material to other material was very much in the latter's favor. The issue of September 10, 1886, had fifteen columns of advertising copy in contrast to thirty of other material.

The *Freie Presse* carried little local matter of the gossipy variety which characterized the German weeklies somewhat later, and particularly after 1900. Its general appearance was very attractive. The spacing, setting of headings, and the proof-reading left little to be desired. It catered also to those who wished to read the local dialect by bringing letters from time to time by *Betzie, Sällie Besenstiel,* and *Der Hansjörg*. And this in spite of its aggressively German tone and its avowed intention to support only the best elements of the German tradition. It emphasized the German character of Berlin and urged its German inhabitants, which in 1887 made up two-thirds of the total population of 6,125 to hold their heads high. It noted editorially that the Germans were a hated people in the world in spite of their peaceful intentions. To combat this hatred, it stated, Germany must become a strong nation in which solidarity reigned: the Germans must be a nation of brothers.

The aggressively German attitude of the *Freie Presse* was perhaps overdone, and its narrow political viewpoint was not justified. The Conservative party which it so ardently supported turned out to be, in the end, the party which suppressed the German newspapers.

In its short career of two years the *Freie Presse* changed editors as well as publishers a number of times. Hett and Buchhaupt, who were the original publishers when the paper appeared on August 6, 1886, had changed to Hett and Waller by October 22 of that year. Heinrich Waller, the new partner, was only twenty-one years of age when he joined Hett on the *Freie Presse*. The former became the editor, while Hett and Company appeared as the publishers. Waller, however, remained only a few months in Berlin, leaving in January 1887 for Milwaukee, Wisconsin. Carl Hartmann became the new editor and M. S. Hallman entered the partnership in the printing establishment. By April 1, 1887, the *Freie Presse Actien-Gesellschaft*, with Adolph Müller as director, had taken over the *Freie Presse*. This company was composed of several prominent local adherents of the Conservative party. Carl Hartmann was to remain as editor. How many subscribers the *Freie Presse* had at this time is not definitely known, but evidently 1000 copies were printed per issue.

In June 1887, Carl Hartmann resigned as editor after serving approximately four months in that capacity. Subsequently Adolph Müller of the Berlin High School staff performed editorial duties. However, in spite of every effort to maintain itself, the *Freie Presse* had to discontinue publication after an existence of approximately two years. Its German competitor in Berlin, the *Berliner Journal*, was jubilant to see this thorn in its flesh disappear, and said so in voluble language.

The *Freie Presse* had attempted to make itself as attractive as possible to the German readers to whom it addressed itself. It provided, as all German weeklies in Ontario, something for everyone. It was well edited and attractively planned. In addition it was intensely German, but the Germans seem not to have supported its determined stand on their behalf. It was becoming evident that the *Freie Presse's* militant attitude was too extreme and out of keeping with the temper of many of the older German immigrants and their descendants who were beginning to feel themselves as part of the whole community, and who were not content to remain a race-conscious minority. In addition, the memories of 1848 had not been completely obliterated by the new glories of the German Empire under Bismarck and William I. There was also a strong undertone of liberalism in the German immigrants which could not subscribe to the pronounced conservative attitude of the *Freie Presse*.

One of the most ambitious of the late-comers in the field of German journalism in Ontario was the *Deutsche Zeitung* of Berlin. The first number of this eight-page weekly appeared on Tuesday, November 3, 1891. It was dedicated to the interests of all the Germans in Canada and purported to be the answer to a long-awaited necessity. The rumor that a new German newspaper was about to appear created considerable flurry at this time among both English and German contemporaries.

It was the product of a group of individuals, mainly local, which actively supported the Conservative party and was to be, therefore, a foil to the *Berliner Journal*, whose political orientation from the beginning of its career until 1904 was strongly Liberal. The group, which initially consisted of local and outside members such as Georg Rumpel (Berlin), Joseph Emm Seagram (Waterloo), H. Meyer (Wingham), John Fennell (Berlin), Charles Cluthe (Toronto), Casper Heller (Berlin), and Henry Gildner (Berlin) counted among its numbers some of the most prominent men in their respective communities. They called their organization *Die Deutsche Druck- und Verlagsgesellschaft von Berlin (Limited)* [The German Printing and Publishing Company of Berlin (Limited)] and named Adolph Müller, who formerly had been associated with the *Freie Presse* in Berlin, as financial secretary, and W. V. Uttley as manager. Michael Scherer, who previously had been foreman in the printing office of the *Waterloo Chronicle*, and subsequently J. H. Schmidt's partner on the *Canadischer Kolonist* in Stratford, and later the editor and publisher of the *Perth Volksfreund* in Stratford and Listowel, was named editor, with F. H. Delion, formerly of the *Elmira Anzeiger* as local editor. In addition, Johann B. Dinkel, formerly local editor of the *Colorado Journal* of Denver, Colorado, joined the staff of the *Deutsche Zeitung*. Dinkel was not a newcomer to German journalism in Ontario, having served as editor of the German section of the *Berlin Daily News* in 1878, and later for some time in a similar capacity on the *Perth Volksfreund* in Listowel.

For a period of slightly more than one year John Fennell was president of the company which published the *Deutsche Zeitung*. He was succeeded by Georg Rumpel in this position. In the early months of 1893, Daniel Hibner of Berlin became a new director in the company.

In December 1893, Michael Scherer's name disappeared as the responsible editor, and no replacement was made until March, 1895, when Hans Sikorski took over the editorial duties. Almost immediately a feud with the *Berliner Journal* began which was, at times, not characterized by too much restraint. The *Deutsche Zeitung* went so far as to state that the *Journal* was not written in proper German. The *Journal* was, however, not the only newspaper to become embroiled in disputes with the newcomer. The English *Berlin Daily News*, the *Canadischer Bauernfreund* of Waterloo, and the *Ontario Glocke* of Walkerton were frequently involved in bitter controversy with the *Deutsche Zeitung*. The *Journal* got more than slight satisfaction out of seeing the last three mentioned newspapers at odds with the *Zeitung* since they were of the same political persuasion as the latter.

The *Deutsche Zeitung* was very active in advertising itself and frequently quoted favorable mention of itself made in other newspapers. It did not hesitate to make its own position and policy clear to the community, on the basis of which it appealed for support.

At the beginning of 1897, the *Deutsche Druck- und Verlagsgesellschaft,* already the owners of the *Deutsche Zeitung* and the *Daily* and *Weekly Record* of Berlin, and the printers of *Das Ottawa Echo,* as well as of the *Kirchenblatt,* the official organ of the Canada Synod of the Lutheran Church, which was previously printed by Otto Pressprich in New Hamburg, also purchased the *Berlin News.* By combining the *News* with the *Record* one of the journalistic competitors in the English language was removed from the local scene.

Das Ottawa Echo, edited and published by A. Drenge, was evidently so short-lived that no information other than a reference to it in the *Deutsche Zeitung* of June 14, 1893, is in existence. It was a monthly of twelve pages with a subscription price of one dollar per year.

On January 7, 1898, the *Deutsche Zeitung,* as well as the *Deutsche Druck- und Verlagsgesellschaft,* suffered a great blow in the sudden death of Adolph Müller, the financial secretary of the company. Born in Scheesel, Hanover, Germany, in 1850, he had come to Canada at the age of nineteen to become later an instructor at the Berlin Grammar School. In addition he was a member of the Hospital Board, of the *Philharmonische Gesellschaft,* and of the Public Library Board. He was a strong supporter of all German activities in Berlin and surrounding areas.

On February 2, 1898, Hans Sikorski resigned as editor of the *Deutsche Zeitung.* Shortly before this time the paper had been slightly enlarged. There were now ten pages which measured 23 1/4 inches high and 16 3/4 inches wide, with seven columns per page. With Sikorski's departure a qualitative disintegration of the *Deutsche Zeitung* becomes apparent. H. Delion, who had been co-publisher of the *Elmira Advertiser,* became the new editor and business manager. He changed the appearance of the newspaper almost immediately, as well as its tone. Advertising material now found its way onto the front page, and brief advertising items were interspersed between news articles and other articles throughout the paper. Patent medicines were heavily represented in this material. There is a further general editorial decline by 1899. At the outset the *Deutsche Zeitung* had prided itself on the fact that it did not rely on the advertising of nostrums and quack remedies to maintain itself, but evidently adverse conditions forced an eventual change of policy.

Suddenly on October 11, 1899, the *Deutsche Zeitung* suspended publication. Its discontinuance left the *Berliner Journal* as the only German newspaper in Berlin, a circumstance which it somewhat belatedly hailed with unfeigned jubilation. However, several years later the name of the *Deutsche Zeitung* was revived when the company which had published it in Berlin purchased the *Canadischer Bauernfreund* in Waterloo. It continued as an amalgamated partner of the *Bauernfreund* until the latter, too, was eventually combined with the *Berliner Journal.*

The general composition of the *Deutsche Zeitung* did not differ radically from its contemporaries. It began with eight pages with six columns per page, the pages measuring 21 1/2 inches high and 15 1/2 inches wide. It was subsequently enlarged both in number of pages and in size, as has been noted above. In material and arrangement, however, the *Deutsche Zeitung* represented, particularly in its early years, a distinct improvement in Ontario German journalism. Its first page, without any advertisements, brought a review of Canadian and European events. Subsequent pages furnished miscellaneous articles with much emphasis on German happenings and personalities in America and elsewhere. Berlin and its environs had a special section, so that the *Deutsche Zeitung* was the first Ontario German newspaper to cater to an increased extent to its own locality. For tidy appearance throughout, clear and legible print, good paper and careful proof-reading, the *Deutsche Zeitung* was a model. It offered more literary material than had heretofore been provided by the German weeklies; six to eight columns per week in the continued story category were common, and the choice of material indicated a desire to present the popular and, to some extent, the better authors of the day. The following random selection will suffice to show the extent and variety of the prose offerings: Ewald August König with *Die Hand der Nemesis* (January 5, 1892 to October 2, 1892), Gustav Freytag with *Soll und Haben* (November 30, 1892 to September 13, 1893). This latter work, Freytag's best novel, was one of the most ambitious attempts ever made by any Ontario German newspaper in presenting a classic in instalment form. The sheer bulk of material monopolized a considerable portion of the *Deutsche Zeitung* every week for forty weeks. Among the less pretentious works are found Woldemar Urban with *Im Banne der Comorra, Sander und Sohn, Im Paradies*, and *Das Gold des Westmoreland*; R. Ortmann with *Unter dem Schwerte der Themis*; Gregor Samarow with *Irrlichter;* Martin Bauer, with *Um den Namen*; Karl Ed. Klopfer with *Das Geheimnis von Birkenried;* Doris Freiin von Spättgen with *Gefährliche Waffen* and *Arbeitskraft*; Otto Elfner with *Tönendes Erz*; and Max Kretzer with *Ein Bettler*.

The poetry column in the *Deutsche Zeitung* was less generous in quantity than in, for example, the *Berliner Journal*. But each issue saw some poems to delight the poetically inclined readers. Johannes Trojan is represented by *Die Saat, Sommer* and *August*, and Hoffmann von Fallersleben by *Dauer im Wechsel*. There are also poems by Friedrich Rückert, Franz von Schönthan, Franz Grillparzer, Friedrich Schlegel, and by a goodly number of anonymous poetizers on a variety of subjects.

In conformity with the avowed policy of the *Deutsche Zeitung* to encourage German cultural activities generally in its constituency, it gave much space in its columns to German musical recitals and performances, to German language study in the schools, and to the German theatre. It also noted with approbation the participation of Germans in the political sphere, or in any other public activity in the community.

Since German music was experiencing a flourishing period in Berlin and the surrounding German community during the 1890's, the reports of musical events loom large in the *Deutsche Zeitung's* chronicle of German cultural manifestations during these years. Thus we discover that *Der Trompeter von Krächzingen*, an operetta, was presented in Waterloo on

June, 13, 1892. According to reports the performance was good. In the same village, *Einer muß heirathen* and *Drunter und drüber* had been played in the theatre on April 18 of the same year. The *Liedertafel*, which had presented the *Trompeter* in Waterloo, gave it in Berlin on September 7, 1892. The German theatre in Toronto presented *Ein Stündchen im Comptoir*, a musical farce in one act by Siegmund Haber, on November 9, 1892. On October 28, 1896, *Faust* was given in English in the Berlin Opera House. The performance was well attended, but the *Deutsche Zeitung* has no words of commendation for the presentation. It could evidently not approve of a translated version of the great German classic. A *Sänger-Picknick* in Berlin on September 1, 1893, attracted a large number of outsiders to the town. On March 26, 1894, the Germans in Toronto dedicated their *Liederkranz-Halle*. On October 11, 12, and 13 of the same year a German *Kirmes* (carnival-fair) was held in Berlin. It proved to be highly popular and drew many visitors to the town. Bismarck's birthday was celebrated by the *Concordia* Singing Society of Berlin, and by the *Harmonie* in Waterloo in 1895. The *Deutsche Zeitung* gave much space to *Das erste Sängerfest des Canadischen Sängerbundes* (The first choral festival of the Canadian Choral Society) held on September 9, 10, and 11, 1895, in Toronto. On November 14, 1895, the *Harmonie* of Waterloo celebrated its first anniversary by repeating *Der Trompeter von Krächzingen*, also offering a second operetta, *Der Freischütz von Kamerun*, on the same program. A much more ambitious *Kirmes* than in 1894 was given in Berlin in 1896. The *Deutsche Zeitung* brought a detailed report accompanied by pictures. The outstanding musical event of the whole period was the celebration of the *Zweites Sängerfest des Canadischen Sängerbundes* (The second choral festival of the Canadian Choral Society) on the 12th and 13th of August, 1897, in Berlin. It was coupled with the unveiling of a monument in the Berlin public park to Emperor William I, of Germany. The *Deutsche Zeitung* used twelve columns to report this event in its issue of August 18, 1897.

German festivals and celebrations anywhere in America were always fully covered, and the rising prowess of Germany in the political, industrial and scientific spheres was extolled. At the same time the *Deutsche Zeitung* noted that the Germans were becoming a hated people because of their successes. An anonymous poem of November 28, 1893, entitled: *Das gehaßteste Volk* (The most hated people), gives a graphic picture of this feeling toward the Germans on the part of their more powerful neighbors, a feeling also shared by the United States. The birthdays of Emperor William II and of Bismarck were specially marked events and, on Bismarck's eightieth birthday on April 1, 1895, greetings were sent by individuals and groups from Berlin and, in addition, a two-page extra was issued by the *Deutsche Zeitung* on March 27, 1895, lauding the character and achievements of this great Prussian statesman.

Coupled with its advocacy of the study of the German language in Ontario schools, the *Deutsche Zeitung* also urged the sons of Germans in Canada to proceed to Germany for advanced studies. It observed that many young Americans were flocking to the German universities, and it implored the children of Canadian Germans to follow that example.

In spite of the insistence on a high standard of German language in the community generally as well as in the newspaper press, the *Deutsche Zeitung* was nevertheless obliged to cater to a certain extent to that portion of its public which desired material in the local dialect. It resisted every inclination to comply with this demand on the part of its readers until January 1897. A series of letters from one *Piet Kickmüller, Bätschler*, began at that time, and appeared at regular intervals thereafter. These letters often filled as much as two columns, and dealt with events of public and private concern in a humorous manner.

A special feature of the *Deutsche Zeitung* was a short column entitled *Müller und Schulze*. It consisted of a dialogue between these two individuals mainly about local happenings. It was initiated in April 1895. Quite often the apparently jocular sentiments expressed by these two gentlemen contained a bitter sting, and on one occasion almost involved the *Deutsche Zeitung* in a libel suit.

The advertising matter during the earlier period of the *Deutsche Zeitung* consisted mainly of professional notices and advertisements of local business and manufacturing firms. Patent medicines were almost completely absent from its advertising columns. The *Deutsche Zeitung* quoted with unconcealed pride a reference to this favorable circumstance which appeared in its English contemporary in Berlin, the *Berlin Record*. The reference, as the *Deutsche Zeitung* provided it for its readers in its issue of April 12, 1893, stated that: "The patronage which the *Deutsche Zeitung* enjoys in regard to its commercial advertising is simply astonishing. The *Zeitung* carries no advertising for quacks, on the contrary only advertisements for reliable business establishments ..." This accolade from the *Record* loses some of its force when one remembers that the same publishing firm that published the *Deutsche Zeitung* also published the *Berlin Record*. As time passed, as has been noted previously, the *Zeitung's* policy underwent a downward revision in this regard. The ratio in quantity of advertising material to the total quantity also underwent a transformation as the quality of the advertising copy deteriorated. In the later period advertising support came from Berlin, Toronto, Hamilton, Bridgeport, and from various other sources.

The *Deutsche Zeitung* almost always ran a distinct editorial column. Here it commented on questions of the day. Frequently it drew on English contemporaries to provide it with a subject on which to base its editorial remarks. A recurring topic was English nativism in Canada, which it combatted with all the vigor it could muster. An example of its attitude is indicated in an editorial of October 30, 1895: "The main purpose of the *Deutsche Zeitung* ist not to create propaganda for any political party. Its main object is to promote German ways and manners, to oppose English nativism and to raise the self-respect of the Germans in Canada. The *Deutsche Zeitung* is German to the core. We therefore hope that the *Deutsche Zeitung* will retain the favor of the German public in the coming year."

It is evident that the attitude of the *Deutsche Zeitung* was too narrowly German, and too politically biased to maintain itself. It continued the tradition of the *Freie Presse* by representing a similar political philosophy, as well as an exaggerated emphasis on the maintenance of the German cultural atmosphere. The Germans in Ontario were rapidly being integrated into the English-dominated pattern, and they also refused to be unduly partisan in their political attitude. A less aggressive approach on the above issues by the *Deutsche Zeitung* might have met with greater approval on the part of the Germans and their descendants. Until the very end of its existence, however, it insisted that it was the largest Canadian-German newspaper and, by implication, the best. It represented the last attempt to begin a new German newspaper in the Waterloo County area.

Remaining as the witness of the appearance and eclipse of more than a score of German newspapers in Ontario was that hardy and persistent perennial, the *Berliner Journal*. It was favored by having a capable and resourceful leadership and a good location in the rapidly-growing town of Berlin, the German stronghold in Western Ontario.

From December 1859 to October 1918 without interruption, it made its way into the homes of an ever-increasing number of subscribers scattered throughout the German communities of Ontario and beyond. There was nothing phenomenal about its growth at any time, but it was steady throughout. According to its own figures it had 1,000 subscribers in 1863, 1,575 in 1873, 1,900 in 1883 and 2,200 in 1893. In May of 1893 it no longer gave circulation figures; instead it laid claim to having a larger number of readers than any other German newspaper appearing in Canada. This claim it never relinquished until the end of its existence.

From December 1859 until December 1880 it was a newspaper of four pages, 26 1/2 inches high and 20 inches wide, with six columns per page. Beginning with January 1881 it had eight pages, reduced in size to 21 1/2 inches high and 15 1/2 inches wide, with six columns per page. In 1904 when the *Ontario Glocke* of Walkerton amalgamated with the *Journal*, the number of pages was increased to twelve and, as the result of further amalgamations in 1909, to sixteen. Until the beginning of the first World War this size prevailed. During this latter period the *Journal* was the only German newspaper still appearing in south-western Ontario. The *Journal* was very popular in its home town, Berlin. In 1894 it noted that 453 of its subscribers lived there.

The *Berliner Journal* began like its German contemporaries in Ontario by being mainly a political newspaper. Foreign political events took up the major bulk of the news space, although local, provincial, Canadian and American political happenings were carefully reported. The European news columns were always headed by Germany, which country received longer and more detailed treatment. The other countries were allotted space as the occasion warranted. Before the completion of the Atlantic cable in 1866, the *Journal* depended on American and English newspapers for provincial and national events. Local items, not of an official nature, were obtained by any method possible, and sometimes hearsay and unconfirmed gossip were presented as fact. Subsequent denials of incorrect reports were not infrequent in the earlier years of the *Journal*. The *Journal* had the good fortune of being moderately well established by the time that events in the United States and in Germany, in approximately the last third of the nineteenth century, began to assume world-wide significance. Among these may be listed the Civil War in the United States, the military campaign by Prussia and Austria against Denmark in 1864, the war between Prussia and Austria in 1866, the Franco-Prussian War of 1870-71, and the subsequent establishment of the German Empire.

In the Civil War in the United States the *Journal* stood wholeheartedly on the side of the Union against the Confederacy. Outstanding Germans who served on the side of the North, particularly Carl Schurz, Franz Sigel and Ludwig Blenker, all of whom became generals in the Union Army, were always in the news. Lincoln was given much space and was hailed as the saviour of the oppressed. There were profuse eulogies at his death and the *Journal* recorded the complete text of the message of condolence sent to the Secretary of State of the United States by a public meeting of 500 Berlin residents, among whom were the town's leading German citizens. Events in the republic across the border were always reported in detail, sometimes state by state. Particularly the relations between Canada and the United States were discussed, including such topics as Fenians, annexation and tariffs. The *Journal* was opposed to annexation, but favored the removal of trade barriers. In doing this, it endorsed the policy of the Liberal party, whose stand on tariffs and other Canadian issues it supported with considerable vigor until 1904. In Canadian affairs, the *Journal* always stood for frugality in public expenditures, and for efficiency in the conduct of public affairs. It followed in detail every major political event in Canada, and was particularly scrupulous about providing full reports on the negotiations which eventually led to the confederation of the provinces in 1867. All proposals and schemes were discussed and commented upon, and editorial opinion concluded that confederation would make Canada a strong country and establish a solid future for it. The plans and events in connection with the celebration of the national holiday on July 1 were always fully reported, and editorial encouragement was given this patriotic event, as well as to the celebration of Queen Victoria's birthday on May 24.[27] The *Journal* interpreted these manifestations as loyal gestures in which its German constituency was playing a major part, even though at times the physical arrangements had a distinctly German flavour.[28]

The careers of Canadian political figures were always followed in detail and, up to 1904, more space was given to those of Liberal than of Conservative persuasion. The *Journal* urged its German readers to be politically active, and to become naturalized Canadians so that they might vote. It outlined the procedure through which one became a British subject, and emphasized the importance of as well as the comparative ease with which the right to exercise the franchise could be achieved in Canada.

Germany and the German-speaking areas in Europe and throughout the world had their activities adequately reported in the *Journal*. The distance from which the *Journal* was permitted to make its observations regarding the fatherland permitted a good measure of objectivity. Prussia was frequently castigated for her militaristic attitude and for her generally illiberal policies. Her restrictive policy concerning press freedom rankled most. The establishment of the Empire under the aegis of Prussia was accepted with an uneasy approval, mainly because it marked an achievement in a long struggle.

The *Journal* gave editorial support to the campaign of the local German Patriotic Relief Society, which was established in 1870, to send contributions to the fatherland. The Franco-Prussian War of 1870-71 was reported in great detail. The interest on the part of many subscribers in the events from the war area was so great that they came many miles on foot, or by vehicle, to procure their copy of the *Journal* at the press. In the summer of 1870 the *Journal* also issued evening extras on several occasions in order to furnish its news-hungry public with the latest war reports. The end of that war was celebrated in Berlin with a peace celebration on May 4, 1871, attended by 10,000 people. The *Kulturkampf*, the Congress of Berlin, the deaths of the first and second German emperors, the accession and subsequent behaviour of William II, and the resignation and retirement of Bismarck were all faithfully chronicled. The deaths of German poets and writers, as well as those of German public figures were always recorded.

By sheer coincidence one of the most critical issues in the new German *Reich*, the *Kulturkampf*, that extended political struggle initiated by Bismarck in 1872, between the German imperial government and the Roman Catholic church concerning control by the state of educational and ecclesiastical appointments, was destined to occupy more space in the *Berliner Journal* than other events that transpired in the new *Reich*. This came about through two personalities, Father Ludwig Funcken, founder of St. Jerome's College, Berlin, Ontario, and Otto Klotz of Preston, a public-spirited and leading figure in that community. The feud between these two men was carried on with much acumen on both sides from September 1872 until May 1873. Klotz strongly espoused the position of Bismarck and argued for a single system of education for the German state. He rejected Father Funcken's contention that a secular system of education smacked of rationalism and godlessness. Historical and philosophical arguments were advanced by both men, but their quarrel, as might be expected, found no resolution in spite of the vigor with which the two opponents addressed themselves to the subject. The controversy did not, however, in any way diminish the warm personal regard the two men had for each other. Funcken's memory still lives on in the educational institution which he began; Otto Klotz served as a justice of the peace and notary public in Preston, became the author of a German grammar for use in the schools, sponsored the Mechanics' Institute in Preston, to which he donated part of his private library and was active in all activities for the betterment of his community. One of his sons, Otto Julius Klotz, after a notable career in various branches of the federal public service, became Dominion astronomer in 1917, a position which he held until his death in 1923.

Public as well as private affairs in England and France, too, loomed large in the week-by-week report. Queen Victoria and the British royal family were constantly in the news, and their close connection to the German reigning houses found frequent mention. The German Emperor's birthday was always celebrated in Berlin as well as Queen Victoria's, but Emperor William I of Germany had a monument erected to his honour in the Berlin, Ontario, public park before a statue to Queen Victoria was placed there. However, the *Journal* advocated a statue to the Queen as the next public project to be undertaken after the unveiling of the Emperor's monument. The cabals and intrigues of Napoleon III were under constant discussion in the news from France before 1870. France's defeat in the war of 1870-71, its subsequent difficulties, the Dreyfus case, and all other major events in that country were kept before the *Journal's* readers.

In fact, the *Journal* overlooked no news items of any importance anywhere in the world. Scandal as an attraction was not rejected as an antidote to the more prosaic events from foreign parts, or even from the more immediate area. Murders, hangings, suicides, poisonings and other sensational happenings were also native to its pages.

The *Journal* was naturally an enthusiastic exponent of the growth and prosperity of its immediate area, Waterloo County, as well as of German-speaking areas everywhere in Ontario. For many years it provided, usually in December, a list of new, repaired or altered structures in Berlin with the monetary value involved. It emphasized the fact that German thrift and inventiveness were rapidly making this town into an important centre of industry in Ontario. The material elements of this prosperity were not subordinated, however, to the cultural advance that proceeded simultaneously. The Journal exhibited great pride in both, urging its German readers to hold their heads high in the knowledge that they were making a worth-while contribution to their adopted country. The part that Germans played in the local political scene and beyond was commended, but it was expected of them that they would further the interests of the German community as such. Failure to do so met with a strong rebuke. A case in point was the stand taken by George Hess, a member of the provincial legislature for North Perth, Ontario, who in the 1880's refused to endorse the teaching of German in the schools of the German communities.

In spite of his stand, however, and largely on account of the strong pressure exerted by the *Journal* and other German newspapers, German language instruction was brought into the elementary and secondary schools in the German communities, and experienced a great flourishing period after 1900, until cut off abruptly by the wave of resentment against everything German that followed almost immediately after the outbreak of the first World War.

In the earlier part of its career the news section of the *Journal* was mainly concerned with political events. Its gradual evolution into a newspaper with a much more pronounced local flavor came when the German pioneers in the community began to die out, thereby cutting the bonds which tied it to the European scene. The trickle of immigrants that came after 1890 into the German communities in Ontario was satisfied by the presentation of some local news from the various German areas in Europe, but the quantity of intimate items submitted by the correspondents from the various German communities it served in Ontario far outweighed the *Lokal-Nachrichten aus der alten Heimath* (Local news from the old homeland) from abroad. The *Journal* noted wistfully that a new order of things was assuming shape as the older German inhabitants were departing this life. The German newspapers generally campaigned even more ardently for the retention of the German tongue as the original settlers passed away. They naturally foresaw the time when there might be no one who could read German. The gradual decrease in the number of readers eventually brought about the amalgamation of the German newspapers in Western Ontario. But even then the appeal was constantly before those who still subscribed to the single remaining newspaper, even as late as 1914, for the Germans whom the *Journal* served, to speak a pure German with their children and their fellow countrymen, and to hold high the German tradition.

But it was difficult for the newspapers to maintain a German outlook in the generation of children of German immigrants who were growing up after 1900. The process of slow fusion was at work, and if country folk might be able to isolate themselves to a degree from their English-speaking neighbors, this was not possible in the villages and towns. There were, naturally, after the last third of the nineteenth century many descendants of German immigrants who were bilingual, but bilingualism is not an inherited trait and can be passed down only in families in which there is sufficient enthusiasm for the second language to have it taught to their offspring. In Berlin, Ontario, the campaign on the part of the German newspapers for German instruction in the schools bore some fruit. In 1900, 166 students took German in the Berlin schools. This number had increased to 800 in 1907, of which 200 came from English homes; to 960 in 1909; and to 1459 in 1913. In September 1915 German instruction was discontinued in the public schools.

The gradual disappearance of a good language standard was met by many of the German newspapers, particularly the *Ontario Glocke* of Walkerton and the *Journal*, by presenting a considerable body of material in the local dialect as well as in Pennsylvania German. The *Berliner Journal*, in fact, began to make this concession to its patronage almost immediately after its establishment. A large number of contributors over many pseudonyms as well as anonymous contributors, writing letters and articles on a multiplicity of topics, fall into this category. *Wunnernahs, Däv, Eisick Schnitzelbank, Sam Beißzang, Sällie Besemstiel, Hansjörk, Soloman der Dumme, Jonathan, Jeremias, Peter Dapper, Der klehn Krämer,*

Johnny Kitzler, John Ritsch, Pit Berastiehl, as well as others, including *Joe Klotzkopp* after amalgamation with the *Ontario Glocke*, made regular appearances in the *Journal*. In time the demand for these features became so imperative that the editors did not dare risk their omission.

Local German music and the German theatre were enthusiastically supported by the *Journal*. The various musical societies, their leaders and sometimes lists of their members, and the programs they presented, were featured in news articles as well as in the occasional advertisement. Criticisms also appeared after performances. These were usually favorable, although the artistic quality of many performances was quite evidently not very high. Thus the *Concordia* and *Orpheus* Singing Societies in Berlin and the *Liedertafel* in Waterloo regularly found mention in the *Journal's* columns. The *Turners*, too and their theatrical troupes, and *Turner* festivals were given strong editorial support. The *Journal* followed the activities of the *Turners* in all the German communities in Canada, with particular emphasis on the *Turner* theatre. The listings here show that the repertoire was not large and generally of the lighter variety.

There were some exceptions to this latter rule, however. The *Journal* brought notice of the following *Turner* theatre performances between 1861 and 1869: *Der Kaiser und der Seiler* by Charlotte Birch-Pfeiffer; *Uriel Acosta* by Karl Gutzkow; *Deborah, die edle Jüdin* by Salomon Mosenthal (guest performance of Madame Schunk of the *Stadt-Theater* in St. Louis as Deborah); and *Der Trunkenbold* by August von Kotzebue. These were all presented by the local *Turner* society.

Immediately after the founding of the German empire, and during the Franco-Prussian War preceding it, the energies of the German people in Ontario were mainly absorbed by political events. By 1874, however, there was a revival of interest in German theatre, although German stage presentations began to be more spasmodic than previously. The *Journal* was pleased at the revival of interest in the German theatre and urged support on the part of the public. The *Turner* theatre was no longer active by this time, and the local theatrical groups were usually an offshoot of the musical societies. The first play in the revival period was *Aufgeschoben ist nicht aufgehoben* by Karl August Görner, on April 6, 1874. There followed *Der Wirrwarr* by Kotzebue; *Lumpazi-Vagabundus* by Johann Nestroy; *Schneider Fips oder die Gefährliche Nachbarschaft* and *Die Zerstreuten*, both by Kotzebue. Kotzebue's *Fremder* and Schiller's *Maria Stuart* were given in Berlin by an outside cast in 1878. After 1880 the local theatrical groups rarely presented a good German play. And by the end of the century the English theatre monopolized the halls where German devotees of *Thalia* had once displayed their talents.

With the gradual decay of the German theatre, so poignantly deplored by the *Journal*, German music came ever more to the fore. The *Journal* now threw all its influence into the support of the musical societies. The *Turners* of Hamilton and Toronto staged music festivals at which the *Journal* urged attendance. The local German societies which attempted to cater to an increased public by having a large part of their program in English found a strong note of disapproval of such a course in the *Journal.* The work of Theodor Zöllner in Berlin, and Heinrich Zöllner in Waterloo, with their choirs, which travelled to the surrounding towns, as well as to Toronto, Hamilton, Ann Arbor, Michigan, and other cities, presenting oratorios and other musical programs, found great favor editorially.

The *Journal* did not, however, fail to continue commenting on the German theatrical offerings even though they had become trifling in quality and sporadic in quantity. It noted an evening performance of the *Dramatischer Verein* on February 24, 1888, at which *Eine Tasse Thee*, a comedy in one act by Franz Drost; *1733 Mark 75 Pfennige*, farce with song by Eduard Jacobson; and *Papa hat's erlaubt* by Gustav von Moser, were presented. A note on March 1, 1888, reported that the performances were good, saying the same also on May 10, 1888, of *Krieg im Frieden*, a military comedy in five acts by Gustav von Moser and Franz von Schönthan. The musical programs were, however, given much more space and commendation, and the *Journal* observed in the autumn of 1888 that Berlin's musical life was becoming more active day by day. Notices of operettas, oratorios and musical programs of every sort to be given, or criticisms after their presentation, are found in almost every issue. Special attention was paid to the great singing festivals that were held annually in one or other of the German communities in Ontario. These festivals were continued until the beginning of the first World War. Music had a distinct advantage over the spoken drama in retaining its appeal. It did not require the vehicle of language in order to be intelligible to the younger generations, whose knowledge of spoken German was beginning to be defective, but whose love of music was as strong as ever.

The literary prose material provided by the *Berliner Journal* was one of its most prominent characteristics. The later German newspapers all laid strong emphasis on this feature, which was designed to provide belletristic matter in a land where German books were difficult to obtain, principally because of a lack of ready cash to pay for them. The weekly newspapers provided this material, in addition to all the other material they contained, for little more than the price of one book per year.

The *Journal,* in common with the other German Ontario newspapers, catered in its literary matter chiefly to the middle and lower intellectual range. This meant that the more outstanding German authors were rarely, if ever, represented in the prose material. Light entertainment, rather than artistic and intellectual excellence, characterizes the prose fiction, as well as the bulk of the poetic material. On the whole this method was better adapted to a moderately literate rather than a highly educated group.

Hundreds of short stories and novels appeared in the *Journal* during the fifty-eight years of its life. Among these were many by writers who remained anonymous, although on several occasions the *Journal* must have been aware of the author's name without, however, troubling to give it. The overwhelming bulk of prose was by contemporary writers. Schiller's *Der Verbrecher aus verlorener Ehre,* which appeared in the summer of 1860, forms an important exception. Some of the more prolific writers of the nineteenth century are represented by as many as six to a dozen works. Among these are Friedrich Gerstäcker, Franz Hoffman, Wilhelm Herchenbach, Bernhard Wörner, J. D. H. Temme, Ewald A. König, Max Ring, Stanislaus Stephen Albert Graf von Grabowski, Gustav Nieritz, Karoline Freifrau von Berlepsch, Julius Uliczny, Herman Hirschfeld, Philipp Laicus, and Walter von Münich. Other writers whose contributions are in more modest proportions are Ludwig Rellstab, Berthold Auerbach, Heinrich Zschokke, Johannes Trojan, Wilhelm Heinrich Riehl, Louise Mühlbach, Ernst Wichert, Otto Ruppius, Balduin Möllhausen, Max Kretzer, Felix Salten, Ernst von Wolzogen, Peter Rosegger, and many other lesser known writers. Otto Ruppius was a *Forty-Eighter* who had come to the United States in 1848 and shortly after had become the editor of the *New Yorker Staatszeitung*. Later, in 1859, he founded the *Westliche Blätter* in St. Louis. In 1861 he returned to Germany, settled in Leipzig, where he wrote many stories about America which became very popular in Germany. He died in 1864. Möllhausen, a venturesome spirit, arrived in America in 1849. He lived with the Indians and accompanied several expeditions to the American West. He became a popular writer of exotic prose in which he depicted mainly American pioneer and Indian life.

When the *Journal* became a twelve-page newspaper, the amount of prose material was considerably increased. Six to eight columns were a usual weekly quota. In this way a full-length novel would appear in serial form in several months. *Die Tochter des Verbannten* by Erich Friesen might serve as an illustration. This novel ran from June 26 to September 18, 1912. In the space of these thirteen weeks a total of 96 1/2 columns appeared in the *Journal*.

There is no doubt that the inclusion of this large bulk of prose material in the *Journal* came in response to popular demand. However, the German newspapers also used it as an advertising feature. They often urged subscribers to be certain to have their subscriptions paid up so as not to miss the next instalment of a gripping tale, and the continued story was also used as bait to attract new subscribers. A large bulk of poetry, too, is to be found in the *Journal*. Its quality is, on the whole, somewhat lower than that of the prose. Local poets loom large, and the many exchanges from far and near which found their way into the *Journal* office made a stately contribution to the ever-present poetry column.

The greatest German poets, then, are rarely represented. Poetry generally had to have entertainment value; or it had to comment on the contemporary scene, both local and foreign, or on changing habits at home and abroad; or it dealt with personalities in the forefront of affairs. *Bindermeyer* and *Bombenmeyer* expatiate on the latest fads in food or clothes, on married life, on bicycles or Bismarck. Literary excellence is not their goal, but morality is frequently the handmaiden of this lowly muse.

Among the well-known German poets Emanuel Geibel, Johann Peter Hebel (whose dialect poems were popular), Ludwig Uhland, Henry Harbaugh (the Pennsylvania-German poet), Ferdinand Freiligrath, Friedrich

Neujahrs-Glückwunsch

der Träger des

Berliner Journal

1872.

Wandkalender für 1872.

Rückert, Friedrich Lexow (a *Forty-Eighter)*, Ludwig Eichrodt, Karl Gerok, Adelbert von Chamisso, Hoffmann von Fallersleben, Joseph Viktor von Scheffel, Friedrich Bodenstedt, Oskar von Redwitz, Georg Herwegh, Rudolf Baumbach, Ludwig Fulda, Johannes Trojan, Annette von Droste-Hülshoff, Robert Reinick, and Wilhelm Hauff are represented. Spread over a period of fifty-eight years, this is not a formidable number, particularly when many of the above were in many instances represented by not more than a poem or two.

Anonymous poetry, the effusions of lesser writers, or of local poets, and conundrums in verse achieved great popularity with *Journal* readers. The titles usually indicate, or at least give some hint of, the contents of this material. A random selection of anonymous poems over the years reveals such titles as: *Rauchen, Schnupfen und Kauen; Heimatlied; Frühlingslied; Das bonapartistische Frankreich; Das ist Yankee-Freiheit; Vergeßt die deutsche Sprache nicht* (this theme finds frequent treatment); *Die deutsche Einigkeit; Deutsche werden wir bleiben; Das deutsche Militärwesen; Der deutsche Bauer; General Moltke; Lob des Sauerkrautes* and untold others. *Biedermeyer* and *Glycerinus Bombenmeyer* provide a running commentary on news and issues of the hour. Usually in a full column they comment on the high cost of living, the yellow press, the haters of Germany, the Darwinians, prize-fighting, the uproar caused by the Shaw-White murder, the family picnic, temperance in America and in Germany, mothers-in-law, drinking, millionaires, singers, nativists and the emperor of Brazil.

Local versifiers, too, made their contribution to the *Journal*. Their outpourings often deal with purely local affairs such as elections, birthday celebrations, deaths and weddings, although some of the more venturesome were led to comment poetically on more world-shaking events. There was in almost all Ontario German newspapers a long poem, presumably by the editor or other member of the editorial staff, to usher in the New Year. This was frequently also issued as a broadside and distributed to the subscribers on behalf of the newspaper carrier who, in return for his faithful and punctual delivery of the newspaper, expected a small gratuity.

These carriers' addresses can lay little claim to literary excellence. Clarence S. Brigham, in *Journals and Journeymen*, gives his opinion on American-English New Year verses:

> The poetry ranges from the veriest doggerel to examples of superior verse, but they do preserve the common opinion on national and local politics, and they often give an insight into the social life of the community.[29]

This is also valid for the Ontario German newspapers. These poems often present opinion on world and local events; make intimate references and allusions; express good wishes to all; beg for continued patronage and prompt payment of the newspaper; and usually end with a request for an unspecified amount of *pourboire* for the carrier. A wall calendar was frequently a part of the broadside flanked by some advertising matter for the issuing newspaper. Frequently these broadsides were artistically adorned with printer's ornaments, although many were plain sheets. Colored paper was also sometimes employed.

Neujahrs-Glückwunsch

der Träger des

Berliner Journal

1888.

Wandkalender für 1888.

The *Journal's* New Year's poem of 1888 was in the local dialect, and may be viewed as an indication of the extent to which purely local considerations dictated that weekly's policies.

The *Journal* did not consistently carry a specific editorial column in its earlier years. Only when the editors strongly felt that they should take a stand on some subject, advanced by some group or individual, or condition existing locally or nationally, did editorial opinion manifest itself. Sometimes a news article had appended editorial comment. Subjects for editorial treatment were the illiberal tendencies of the ruling group in Germany; the prevalence of crime in Canada; the inordinate urge to build railroads; the union of the Canadas; naturalization laws; the benefits of life insurance; scandals and waste in government; the excessive cost of maintaining a governor-general; high tariffs and free trade; the platform of the Liberal party; pleas for the retention of the German language in Ontario German communities; the insignificant role played by the Germans in Canadian politics; and, at the very end of the *Journal's* career, pleas for the Germans here to remain calm when the first World War came. The editorialized news article was not a feature peculiar only to the *Journal* among the German newspapers of Ontario. It shared this characteristic with its German as well as English contemporaries of the day.

The *Journal* always carried a considerable quantity of advertising material. Local merchants were well represented. The *Journal,* however, did not spurn any advertising material that yielded income. Consequently, patent medicines loom large in the advertising columns. Short advertising items are frequently strewn among news items and often had a headline which was designed to catch the eye of the unwary reader, who found himself well within the article before he realized that it was an advertisement, usually of a liniment or a pain-killer. This particular method of advertising has not been abandoned in our day, even by the better daily newspapers. The *Journal* furnished free of charge notices of births, deaths, prices of farm products, railway schedules and official notices, as a public service.

The feuds between rival newspapers which were a common characteristic of the fourth estate in the nineteenth century also had their echo in the *Journal.* The *Deutscher Canadier* was the object of its displeasure during the *Journal's* early years, particularly because it was its chief competitor in Berlin. Later local competitors, such as the *Freie Presse* and the *Deutsche Zeitung* were given little favorable comment. It is evident that editors in the nineteenth century subscribed to the theory that the best defence was attack, and used that technique frequently in dealing with their rivals. The *Journal* always seemed to win its verbal battles in which, incidentally, it never sank to improprieties, although it did not shrink from using sharp words when aroused. The defeat of a rival created no remorse in the firm of Rittinger and Motz. The *Journal* wished to be, and also to have the reputation of being, the best German newspaper in Canada. It was sensitive to references made to it elsewhere, and was delighted to be able to quote quite early in its career a Berlin, Germany, newspaper which had made some flattering remarks about it. Under the heading of *Was man in Preußisch-Berlin über Canadisch-Berlin sagt* (What is said in Berlin, Prussia, about Berlin, Canada) it quotes the *Deutsche Roman-Zeitung*, on August 5, 1869, as follows:

First and foremost in the *Berliner Journal*, published by Rittinger and Motz with a motto from Schiller: *Wahrheit gegen Freund und Feind* (Truth alike toward friend and foe), we have a newspaper in the vast format of "paper *ad infinitum.*" It indicates, at least in its outward appearance that our country village namesake on Lake Ontario has doubtless the makings of a metropolis in itself. — But the German-American Berliners are practical. That comes immediately to light through the fact that the first three columns of the *Journal* are filled with advertisements, which are then followed by the belletristic section. From the former we note with satisfaction that this Berlin also has a *Königstraße* (King Street), and that Petersburg and Strassburg reach out a neighbourly hand to the little town. As regards the extolling of fabulously cheap clothing, various other wares, patent medicines, etc., it yields nothing to us. In the manner of presentation of such advertising material the metropolis of our North German intelligence lags considerably behind that of "New Germany" on Lake Ontario, e.g.: "Colossal rush for cheap goods; cheap woollen blankets are the order of the day. Come directly to my store. I manufacture the best wool blankets in the Dominion and sell them at wholesale prices. The overhead in my business is low: no rent to pay, no profit to share, no partners in my business, and since I import all my goods directly, one can buy good and cheap goods at my place. Visit me before you buy elsewhere. I am convinced that you will save 15 per cent if you shop at my store." And an enormous illustration indicates that this colossal rush is directed toward the *Goldener Löwe* (Golden Lion). Another merchant advertises under the sign of "Facts for the people" and offers cheap hardware for sale. This can be procured at the *Goldene Zirkelsäge* (Golden Circular Saw). Even more practical is a photographer who admonishes the readers: "Have your picture taken while you are still pretty." That the *Journal* then too brings a *Novelle* by Louise Mühlbach will certainly surprise no one. A short very clearly written review follows with items from Europe. A serious, if somewhat high-flown article reminds the readers of the Christmas festival and its significance, in which it at the same time—practical as always—alludes to the example of the founder of the Christian religion to abate want and alleviate suffering. Comprehensive reports about lynch law in Indiana, the proceedings of the town council, a note about elections, and the details of a hanging fill the remaining pages. All this is skillfully written in an elevated style. The latter news item contains a very aptly supported argument against capital punishment. In the middle of this material there appears a list of the new advertisements with the reminder that the *Journal* has a circulation of 1500, and is consequently a good advertising medium. Then follows an invitation, just as in Prussia, to subscribe for the coming year, which closes with the words: "We do not promise much, but will try to accomplish all the more." To complete the characteristically naive tone of the article is the appended greeting: "According to established custom the *Journal* will not appear next week in order that our staff may at least once a year shake off the accumulated grime, get a breath of fresh air and enjoy a bit of relaxation."

The *Journal* corrected the *Roman-Zeitung* for its lack of knowledge of Ontario geography by pointing out that Berlin was not situated on Lake Ontario.

The *Journal's* new format in January 1881 brought favorable comment from its German contemporaries in Ontario, as well as from *Die Stimme der Wahrheit* in Detroit, and the Milwaukee *Herold*. Two Ontario English newspapers, the Toronto *Globe* and the *Berlin Daily News*, also extended felicitations. Again in 1883 it spotted a reference to itself in the Toronto *Globe* which it promptly provided in translation for its readers.

The *Journal* had become by 1900 the pre-eminent German newspaper in Ontario. It was logical that any further development in the history of that press should be closely associated with the future of the *Journal* itself, because of its strategic location and energetic leadership.

In the year 1901, shortly before the amalgamation of the German newspapers in south-western Ontario began in earnest, a German weekly was established at Arnprior, in Renfrew County. After a career of five years in that village, it was moved to the more populous centre of Pembroke. The German settlements in this area of Ontario, which had begun in the 1850's, had by the turn of the century, reached considerable proportions, with close to 10,000 German-speaking people within Renfrew County and its bordering municipalities.

The *Deutsche Post*, as the newspaper was called, had as its originator a Lutheran pastor, Bahne Peter Christiansen. He was both its editor and publisher. He addressed himself with vigor to the German community which he intended so serve and pointed out that the *Deutsche Post* was the only German weekly newspaper in eastern Ontario and Quebec. It was consequently recommended as a first class advertising medium for that part of the country. The particular areas to which he appealed for support were Renfrew County; the city of Ottawa; Montreal and Ladysmith in the province of Quebec; and the Parry Sound District of New Ontario. In politics the *Deutsche Post* was independent.

The *Post* began as an eight-page paper of six columns per page and measured 22 inches high and 15 inches wide. Its subscription price was one dollar per annum. By 1911 the annual subscription had been increased to $ 1.50. This increase in price coincided with an increase in the size of the newspaper from eight to twelve pages.

The popularity of the *Post* is indicated by its rapid growth. It very quickly had 600 subscribers and passed the 1,000 mark by 1905. It reached its high point in circulation during 1912 and 1913, when 1,400 copies were distributed. The beginning of the first World War saw some decline in circulation and in 1916 the *Post* seems to have suspended publication.

B. P. Christiansen, its first editor and publisher, died on December 2, 1908, at the age of forty-five years. He was succeeded by Emil B. Christiansen, his son, who remained with the *Post* until it ceased to appear.

The *Deutsche Post* attracted little notice in German circles in Western Ontario which were, journalistically, well served by the *Berliner Journal* and associated weeklies. Gotthard Maron, in his "Die Deutschen in Canada", in *Der Nordwesten- Kalender für das Jahr 1914*, noted its existence in that year without, however, giving any details.[30] Two years later it was to succumb to the feeling of resentment against all things German in Canada which followed in the wake of the outbreak of the war.

Leo J. Kiefer — Hermann Rittinger — William J. Motz — John Motz — Frederick Rittinger — John Treusch — William Rittinger

Berliner Journal Printing Office, King Street West, Berlin, Ontario. About 1889.

RITTINGER & MOTZ
GERMAN
BERLINER JOURNAL
WALKERTON GLOCKE
JOB
PRINTING

CHAPTER IV
THE PERIOD OF AMALGAMATION, 1900—1909

It was becoming increasingly evident after 1900 that there were too many German newspapers for the size of the German-speaking community in Ontario. The costs of publication of a German newspaper were higher than those of an English one. There were several reasons for this. German type was more expensive than English type; German newspapers could not use the "patent" insides used by many English newspapers, particularly the weeklies; the German newspapers were obliged to pay higher wages to their printing staffs than their English contemporaries as the supply of German printers was smaller and therefore the resulting competition for their services greater. The results of these higher costs were that the subscription price of German weeklies was usually somewhat higher than that of the English weekly newspapers.

The higher subscription rates were, however, only one of several reasons for the slowly decreasing subscription lists of the German newspapers after 1900. Fusion and assimilation of the German group into the English-speaking community presented a much greater threat to the continuation of the German newspaper press. The second and third generations of German-Canadians were not moved by the argument to preserve the German language as their immediate forbears had been, in spite of the persistent plea of the German newspapers to do so.

After 1900, then, a period of amalgamation of the remaining German newspapers began. The first major amalgamation came in 1904 when the *Ontario Glocke* of Walkerton joined hands with the *Berliner Journal* of Berlin. The main reason advanced for this move was to maintain the strength of the German press. The price of the new paper was not increased, although the size was changed from eight to twelve pages. Both the *Journal* and the *Glocke* mastheads were retained in order not to offend the old subscribers, but the content of both papers was identical.

The editorial reorganization following this step saw William J. Motz, son of John Motz, as local editor; Herman Rittinger as mechanical supervisor; and John A. Rittinger, formerly editor and publisher of the *Ontario Glocke*, as political and responsible editor of the combined papers. Herman and John A. Rittinger were the sons of Friedrich Rittinger, who had died in 1897, and who was the original partner of John Motz on the *Journal*. A distinct improvement in every department becomes evident after the amalgamation of these two papers. Although the *Journal-Glocke* thereafter became independent in politics, it nevertheless engaged in a vigorous discussion of contemporary political issues in its editorial columns. Six hundred new subscribers were added in the first year after amalgamation. According to an advertisement in a business directory for

1906, the combined circulation of the *Journal* and *Glocke* was 3,900 subscribers.[1]

On July 1, 1906, the *Canadischer Kolonist* of Stratford amalgamated with the *Journal-Glocke.* J. H. Schmidt, the former editor of the *Kolonist,* remained as agent and correspondent in Stratford. The subscription list of the *Kolonist* had shrunk to about 800 by that time. Schmidt gave as reasons for his course his age, the cost of a new type-setting machine, and the difficulty of obtaining a German type-setter. The Toronto *Globe* ascribed the failure of the *Kolonist* to the disappearance of the German language in the Stratford area. This statement was vigorously denied by the *Journal* which claimed that more German was spoken at that time in Western Ontario than twenty-five years previously.

These amalgamations had the effect of changing the nature of the conglomerate product in contrast to their former individual character. An attempt was not made to satisfy the various communities served previously by the individual newspapers and, in truth, the whole German community in Ontario. The new newspaper became much more intimate in tone and carried a large body of local news which reduced the former more literary quality of the *Journal* and, although its appeal as a news-disseminating agent was widened, its level as a cultural vehicle was somewhat reduced. European political news was no longer given the priority it once enjoyed. Local gossip from the German areas in Europe had begun to take its place. This material was carried under the heading of *Lokal-Nachrichten aus der alten Heimath* and frequently filled three complete columns in the *Journal.*

On December 2, 1908, the *Canadisches Volksblatt* amalgamated with the *Canadischer Bauernfreund* of Waterloo. On July 1 of the following year the *Bauernfreund* passed into the hands of Rittinger and Motz. Andreas Weidenhammer, the last editor of the *Bauernfreund,* was retained in Waterloo as agent and correspondent. All the German papers in Ontario, with the exception of the *Deutsche Post* of Pembroke, were now in the possession of the firm of Rittinger and Motz. The amalgamated papers were issued under a different number of mastheads in order that old subscribers would not miss the familiar heading which many of them had seen for scores of years.

CHAPTER V
THE CRITICAL YEARS, 1909—1918

The last phase (1909-1918) of pioneer German journalism in Ontario, then, saw the second generation of the families of Rittinger and Motz, the founders of the *Berliner Journal*, as the sole publishers and editors of a German newspaper in south-western Ontario, even though the fiction of several was preserved by issuing it under several different captions. The future for this firm looked secure, but for one thing. That was something over which it had no control, as its focal point lay not in Canada, but in Europe: the threat of war between Germany and England. The German newspapers in Ontario had faithfully chronicled the events that led to the estrangement of these two countries, but like something that takes place in an area so remote that they could never be affected by its ramifications; and although occasionally the enmity of the two countries evoked a feeling of fear, the German newspapers seemed to feel that war between England and Germany would be impossible.

The campaign to bring German into the schools of Berlin had borne good results. German was still the language of the main service in many churches in the German communities. German music maintained its position under the sponsorship of singing and musical societies and it had the wholehearted support of the *Journal* and its satellites. The local dialect was, however, superseding the standard language more and more. The *Journal* had slowly become a quite thoroughly Canadian paper published in the German language.

Circulation figures from 1909 until 1918 show a small but steady decline in the number of subscribers of the amalgamated newspapers. The average sworn circulation for the year ending December 31, 1909, was 5,154. [1]

By the following year this had shrunk to 5,075. [2] Yearly figures from 1911 to the time of suspension of publication reveal the following pattern: 1911 — 4,806; 1912 — 4,480; 1913 — 4,314; 1914 — 4,419; 1915 — 4,029; 1916 — 3,986; 1917 — 3,451; and 1918 — 3,198. [3] A glance at these figures shows a loss of approximately 2,000 subscribers in the last nine years of publication.

Herman Rittinger died on September 22, 1913; John A. Rittinger on July 29, 1915. In the meantime the first World War had broken out. The *Journal* pleaded with the Germans in Canada to remain calm and to remember their duty to their adopted country. It had great difficulty, however, in satisfying its reading public, being either too patriotic or not enough, too English or too German. All war news was faithfully reported according to the official dispatches. But a heavy cloud rested over the formerly sprightly *Journal*. In September, 1915, there was a reorganization of the company, necessitated by the passing of John A. Rittinger. W. J. Motz became president, W. H. Schmalz vice-president, and C. C. Johannes Maass editor. By March, 1916, the Rittinger and Motz name disappeared from the main caption on the first page, and the *Journal* sank into the anonymity of being "printed and published in Canada." On September 6, 1916, the name "Berlin" disappeared on the *Journal's* date-line and "Kitchener", as the town was now called, was substituted. Even before then, on May 31, 1916, the *Journal* was reduced in size to eight pages instead of the usual twelve, although this reduction was not consistently adhered to. Local dialect letters under two headings, *Brief vum Lex* and *Brief vum Liewei*, continued. Poetry and humor almost completely disappeared. The continued story still flourished. The Christmas number of December 20, 1916, sought to be an echo of former days, but it lacked the enthusiasm which once marked its holiday number. On January 10, 1917, the name *Berliner Journal* made way for a new name, the *Ontario Journal*. An occasional poem, the work of the editor, and simply signed C. C. J. M., was the only poetry that appeared in it at this time. Editorial comment practically vanished. The war news that appeared chronicled the slow but inevitable disintegration of German military resistance; with that collapse came also the final scene for the German *Journal* itself. A new linotype machine, which could set both English and German type, was procured in the autumn of 1918. The announcement of its purchase on October 2, 1918, coincided with an Order-in-Council issued by the cabinet of the government of Canada prohibiting newspapers in the German language in Canada. The *Journal* was obliged to abide by this decree, although government authorities admitted that its attitude during the war had been scrupulously correct.

October 2, 1918, marks the end of the pioneer phase of German journalism in Ontario. The revocation of the Order-in-Council at a later date did not bring about any immediate revival of the German newspaper press in the province. Fusion and assimilation of the German community into the predominantly English-speaking pattern precluded any attempt to re-establish the German newspaper, which for eighty-three years had given information, joy and comfort to immigrants from the German lands who came to Ontario unequipped to read English newspapers.

What a Canadian historian says regarding the importance of the early English periodicals of Upper Canada generally applies to the pioneer German newspapers as well when he states that:

> The value of these periodicals to the historian has not always been appreciated. They contain virtually the only accounts of the debates in parliament published prior to the establishment of the Canadian *Hansard* in 1872; they are almost the sole source of information with regard to the criminal trials of an earlier day; the advertisements and market news contained in them provide the economic historian with data to be found nowhere else; the notices of deaths, births, and marriages are essential to the biographer and the genealogist, unless he is prepared to search tombstones; and the bibliographer must rely on them, not only for notices of publications otherwise unknown, but also for an understanding of the general background of his work. Old newspapers yield place neither to books nor to manuscript materials as a source of information regarding the past. [4]

CHAPTER VI
FINALE AND RETROSPECT

An examination of the extant files furnishes ample evidence to establish the importance of the part played by the German newspaper press in the Ontario German communities, in the period from 1835 to 1918.

The first task of the German newspapers was to provide their German reading public with a weekly review of significant domestic and foreign events. Implicit in this task was some interpretation of these events in editorial form. The German newspapers were sensitive to the fact that they represented a minority group and, as spokesmen of opinion, they articulated the desires and feelings of that group. At the same time they were also media through which opinion was exerted on their clientèle. They were very jealous of their position in relation to their English contemporaries as news-gathering and interpreting organs, and placed great emphasis on their reliability as molders of thought, although they admitted that at times they were tardier than their English rivals in reporting the news.[1] However, news coverage was usually adequate and basically objective.

Heinz Lehmann's observation in his article "Deutsche Zeitung für Canada" of September 1935 concerning the prime function of the Ontario German newspapers is fundamentally valid when he states that "no matter how primitive the printing establishments, nor how completely insignificant the contents were in general, all of the German newspapers faithfully performed one important task: the reporting of events in Germany. In this way they kept their readers in constant spiritual contact with their homeland. Only the widespread desire for news from their homeland made it possible for so many newspapers to exist contemporaneously".[2]

Although a semblance of spiritual contact with Germany was maintained by newspapers, a predominantly Canadian character also manifested itself early in their development. This early preoccupation on the part of the German newspapers with the Canadian scene was a prelude to the process of fusion and assimilation of the German minority, which was, in turn, conditioned to a large extent by the composition of the German settlements, in which it was difficult to maintain the element of racial solidarity because of lack of intellectual leadership. Alexander J. Schem could say in the *Deutsch-Amerikanisches Conversations-Lexicon* of 1871 that "if the Germans [in Canada] make their presence felt to a much lesser degree than their kinsmen in the United States, the chief reason lies in the fact that educated German families occur only in scattered and isolated instances in the Dominion, and that the great majority of the Germans belongs to the lower social classes."[3]

While it is true that farmers and artisans formed the bulk of the German migration to Ontario, these groups were not so illiterate as is sometimes assumed by critics from the fatherland. The large quantity of literary material offered by the German press furnishes an eloquent denial to a lack of interest in cultural matter.
It is, nevertheless, a fact that the Germans in eastern Canada never produced a single individual, with the possible exception of Sir Adam Beck, who might have appeared as their spiritual mentor. But he came too late and in addition lacked any inclination to essay such a role. There was also no migration of *Forty-Eighters* into Canada. Heinz Lehmann's dictum that "the stream of educated individuals from Germany which migrated to the United States after 1848, and there became the leaders of the German community, found no counterpart in Canada, so that there was here always a complete lack of intellectual leaders from their own circles" [4], must be accepted as essentially correct. The corollary then is inescapable that the Germans in Ontario as a group exerted little influence on the course of events in that province. A lack of sufficient concentration of German population in the aggregate as well as in specific areas, with the possible exception of Waterloo County, precluded group action at any time.
On the other hand this scattering also preserved the Germans in Ontario from an extended period of cultural isolation and colonial petrification which Ernst Feise propounds as a characteristic of the German-Americans. [5] The Germans were drawn so rapidly into the English-dominated pattern in Ontario that the petrification process never became very apparent. A ruling of the provincial department of education in 1890, whereby English was made the obligatory language of elementary school instruction, hastened the break-down of the German tradition. It might be said that the Germans in Ontario yielded to the pattern that evolved out of the mixture of races in Ontario, and that the end-product represents not a petrification stage of any one language or racial group, but of the composite mass. Houses, furniture, manners, clothing, books and food yield scarcely any clue as to the original racial background of the inhabitants of the various areas. Surnames are almost the only distinguishing characteristic.
It was natural that the German newspaper press, for purely selfish reasons, should resist the weakening of the German tradition among its patronage. This explains its unrelenting insistence on German reading, singing, language study, and on the retention of German customs generally. In retrospect it becomes evident that this insistence was in the best interest of the German immigrant, since it spared him the misfortune of being plunged precipitously into a cultural vacuum.
In this regard the German newspaper press of Ontario played a rôle comparable to that of German journalism in the United States. Albert Bernhardt Faust eloquently sums up this rôle when he concludes that:

A province bordering on German-American literature is German-American journalism . . . The great function of German journalism in America, viewed historically, has been to prepare the German population for good citizenship. German newspapers have accelerated the process of assimilation by interesting their foreign-born readers in American politics, history, and present conditions. Secondly, they have exerted a conservative influence on their patronage by upholding the German language, and increasing their pride in German culture and civilization. The German newspapers . . . have been strongly patriotic in all matters concerning national or local politics; they [were] German or conservative only on questions of language and culture. [6]

The presence of two somewhat distinct groups of German settlers in Ontario, those who came from Pennsylvania and those who came subsequently directly from Germany, complicated the problem of maintaining an aggressive German attitude on the part of the German press. The settlers from Pennsylvania brought their dialect to which the immigrants from the fatherland adjusted themselves. This had the tendency to nullify the effort on the part of the German newspaper editors, who were almost in every case from Germany itself, or the sons of immigrants from that quarter, to maintain a good standard of language. The editors, then, responded to the presence of both groups, but the trend, since there were no powerful corrective influences in the German community, was away from the best standard. As time went on, the concessions made to the local dialect became more pronounced and little effort was made to stem it, beyond that of persuasion and protest.

Sentimental manifestations to the German fatherland were fervently supported by the majority of German newspapers, but the pleas often fell on ears that were deaf to their pleas.

The German newspapers without exception were aware that they could not maintain a foreign outlook in their readers. To be in Canada and not of Canada would have been foreign to the German character which desires to be noticed and appreciated by those among whom it casts its lot. It was this urge to adapt itself which brought about the fusion of the German group into the local pattern. The newspapers often gave expression to the strong feeling toward their adopted country which animated many of the German immigrants, and which is, perhaps, best exemplified by Dr. August Kaiser's patriotic hymn entitled *Canada*.

Dr. Kaiser was born in St. Agatha in 1843, and died in Detroit in 1894. He became a well-known physician in Detroit, but in addition to his medical work found time to enter city politics there, becoming first an alderman and later president of the board of aldermen. Dr. Kaiser left no doubt as to his own racial origin, for the melody to which his hymn was set was "Die Wacht am Rhein". It was reproduced in the various German weeklies of the time, and even in translation retains its sentiments undiminished.

CANADA

O Canada, thou beauteous land,
Thou art my treasured fatherland.
To thee eternal troth I'll swear,
E'en though in foreign lands I fare.
    Dear Canada, thou beauteous land
    Dear Canada, thou Freedom's strand.
    Thou art fore'er my lovéd fatherland,
    Thou art fore'er my treasured fatherland.

II

Thou Canada, so great and free,
Art rich indeed, O hail to thee.
Hast gold and silver, iron, ore,
Corn, wheat and grain from shore to shore.
Dear Canada, thou beauteous land, etc.

III

In accents loud I say to all,
That thou hast laws — in number small —
The best that man hath yet ordained,
Thou giv'st thy people unconstrained.
Dear Canada, thou beauteous land, etc.

IV

All hail to thee, belovéd land,
Thou art fore'er my fatherland.
Though lordly be the foreign shore,
Thou hast my love for evermore.
Dear Canada, thou beauteous land, etc. [7)]

The passing of the pioneer German newspaper press in Ontario must be deplored, and its prohibition, in retrospect, seems to have been hasty and ill-advised. A language in itself does not create disloyalty, even if it is at the moment the language of the enemy. The German press of Ontario had through more than eighty years of existence demonstrated its loyalty to Canada and to British institutions, and its suppression almost at the very end of the first World War seemed unnecessary. Its continuation would have added a relieving touch of color to a province which was sombre enough, but whose ideal seemed at that stage to be that of conformity and homogeneity.

CHAPTER VII
THE FUTURE

The antipathy engendered by the first World War against all things German died down slowly in Canada, and particularly so in English-speaking eastern Canada, which, in the main until relatively recent times, has indicated under-currents of resentment against people who had not migrated to it from the United Kingdom, or who had not remained loyal to the British tradition during the American Revolution.

The German newspaper press was, consequently, not revived in eastern Canada after the prohibition imposed on it was lifted after the first World War. In January 1920 newspapers in the German language were again allowed to circulate. The revival of the German press came in western Canada, which has had almost from the earliest beginnings a much more heterogeneous and cosmopolitan population than the east. By 1921 the four German newspapers in western Canada that had resumed publication had a circulation of approximately 40,000. Among their subscribers were no doubt some recruited from eastern Canada, as is evidenced by the news coverage which was intended to increase their appeal to the eastern German-Canadian.

But integration and fusion into the English-speaking pattern — the hazard of all minority newspapers — continued to operate. By 1931, in spite of considerable German immigration after 1923, the combined circulation of the German weeklies had shrunk to 26,000. In the year 1921 approximately every sixth German-Canadian read a German newspaper. By 1931 only one in every twenty subscribed to a German weekly. More than seventy per cent of the people of German extraction gave English as their mother tongue in 1931, out of a total of approximately 600,000 people of German name.

Between the first and second World Wars the German newspaper press maintained itself only with difficulty. Added to its other difficulties was the incidence of the depression and its blighting effect on the agricultural economy of western Canada, from which it drew most of its support.

In response to political undercurrents of the day, publications of the extreme left and the extreme right made their appearance. They were short-lived, however, and disappeared with the outbreak of the second World War. During the second World War German newspapers circulated without let or hindrance in Canada. This generous gesture marked a distinct change in government policy from that followed in the first World War.

The subscription lists of all Canadian German newspapers, in spite of vigorous campaigns to draw the Canadians of German extraction into their fold, made little progress in the decade before 1939. What had happened previously in Ontario in the nineteenth and early twentieth centuries was now taking place in western Canada: rapid fusion and integration of the German racial groups.

The end of the second World War brought revelations of National Socialist behavior that shocked even the most fair-minded Canadians. But events subsequent to the great conflict forced the former enemies of Germany to reassess their avowed plans for the future of that unhappy land. Among these were the opening of the gates to immigrants to Canada several years after the cessation of hostilities. By 1956 approximately 220,000 new German immigrants had come to Canada. The German newspapers could look forward to thousands of new readers. This hope came to fruition. But it soon became evident that the Canadian German newspapers did not appeal to the post-war arrivals. They found the German newspapers in Canada but weak and anemic counterparts of the newspapers produced in their European homelands. The newspapers made a heroic effort to accommodate themselves to the new subscribers. Some improvement in the technical aspects of production as well as in general tenor became evident, but it was too much to expect of the Canadian German newspapers to achieve a standard equal to one of the better European newspapers of the German-speaking lands.

The province of Ontario, and in particular the city of Toronto, has attracted the greatest number of post-war immigrants. If Toronto could not, or would not, support a German weekly in the first phase of German journalism, that situation has now changed. Toronto now has a German newspaper, and even Montreal in the heart of French Canada has its own German weekly. It is significant that Kitchener, which as Berlin was the focal point of German journalism in the earlier phase, has not had a German newspaper since 1918.

What is eventually in store for the German newspapers of the second phase cannot be stated with any certainty. That an attempt will be made to keep them alive as long as possible may be accepted as a fervent desire on the part of both the publishers and those readers who still find comfort and consolation in the German language. But the final story of the second phase, though delayed perhaps, cannot differ greatly from that of the first one. The processes of fusion and integration of the German immigrants has proceeded apace, because of the fact that there has been built up in the most recent migration no rallying area for the German group, such as Waterloo County provided in the nineteenth and early twentieth centuries.

It is evident that the German newspapers are aware of their ultimate difficulties. The competition among them is keen, and is bound to become more intense as the subscribers and advertisers diminish in numbers. Immigration, which would have supplied a steady stream of new readers, has been reduced to a trickle. The situation of 1900 and after during the first flourishing period of German weeklies in Canada may soon be reached. In the meantime the largest ones, *Der Nordwesten* established in Winnipeg in 1889, and *Der Courier* established in Regina in 1907, are maintaining themselves.

It will be the duty of some later historian to chronicle the fate and fortune of the second phase of German journalism in Canada.

BIOGRAPHICAL NOTES AND OTHER RELEVANT MATERIAL

(The translations throughout the work are by the author).

CHAPTER I

1 Stewart, J. J., "Early Journalism in Nova Scotia," *Collections of the Nova Scotia Historical Society*, 1887—1888. Halifax, 1888, VI, 91—122.

2 Taubert, Sigfred, "Die frühesten deutschen Drucker in Canada," *Börsenblatt für den Deutschen Buchhandel*—Frankfurter Ausgabe—Nr. 38 a, 14. Mai, 1956, pp. 649—650.

3 Thomas, Isaiah, LL. D., *The History of Printing in America*. Albany, N. Y.: Joel Munsell, 1874. Vol. 1, pp. 357—360.

CHAPTER II

1 List of the subscribers to the *Canada Museum und Allgemeine Zeitung*. The payments made either in whole or part are indicated. A blank of course indicated no payment. According to the announcement of August 27, 1835, the names of the subscribers were put in alphabetical order to avoid any show of partiality:

Bamberger, Peter	20 Thaler	bezahlt
Bauman, Benjamin	20	bez. 10
Bauman, Heinrich B.	20	
Bauman, Jonathan B.	20	bez. 3
Bauman, Samuel	20	bez. 5
Bechtel, Johann	20	bezahlt
Bechtel, Levi	20	
Benner, Jacob	20	
Brubacher, Johannes	20	bezahlt
Brücker, Samuel	20	bezahlt
Devitt, Barnabas	20	bez. 10
Eby, Benjamin	40	bezahlt
Eby, Isaak	20	bezahlt
Van Egmond, Anton	40	
Erb, Daniel	20	bez. 14 u. 80 cts.
Erb, Peter	20	bez. 15
Erb, Joseph	20	bezahlt
Erb, Johannes	20	bez. 10
Eschelmann, Johannes	20	bezahlt
Gaukel, Friedrich	20	bez. 12
Gilkison, David	20	
Guth, David	20	bez. 5
Huber, Peter	20	
Kinsie, Joseph	20	bezahlt
Lichty, Johannes	20	bezahlt
Martin, Daniel	20	
Martin, David	20	bez. 10
Martin, Heinrich	20	bez. 12
Martin, Johannes	20	bezahlt
Martin, Joseph C.	20	bez. 10
Musselmann, David	20	bez. 15
Reist, David	20	
Schantz, Christian, Jr.	30	bezahlt
Schantz, Christian	20	bezahlt
Schantz, Jacob	20	bezahlt
Schantz, Jacob, Jun.	20	bezahlt
Schantz, Joseph	20	bez. 5
Schantz, Isaak	20	bez. 10
Schneider, Jacob C.	40	bezahlt

Schneider, Joseph, Sr.	20	bezahlt
Schumacher, Jacob S.	20	bezahlt
Schumacher, Jacob, Sen.	20	bezahlt
Urmy, Isaak	20	bezahlt
Wanner, Heinrich	20	bezahlt
Weber, Abraham	20	bezahlt
Weber, David	20	bez. 10
Weber, Heinrich	20	bez. 10
Weber, Daniel	20	
Weber, Moses	20	bezahlt
Weber, Benjamin	20	bez. 10
Wißler, Johannes	20	bez. 10

[2] Motto of the *Canada Museum und Allgemeine Zeitung*, August 27, 1835:

Allgemein wie der Sonnenschein,
Sey diese Zeitung Allgemein.
Aus der Nähe — aus der Ferne,
Bringend alles Neue gerne.

Translation:

As far as shines the sun's bright light,
Shall ring our message clear and bright;
From local scenes, as from afar,
It brings its news to where you are.

[3] Peterson's farewell to the readers of the *Canada Museum und Allgemeine Zeitung*, December 18, 1840:

Freunde, lebet wohl.
Museum Leser, lebet wohl.
Feinde, hab' ich deren, lebet wohl.
Alles zeitliche hat ein Ende.

Translation:

Friends, farewell.
Museum readers, farewell.
Enemies, have I any, farewell.
All things temporal come to an end.

[4] *Canada Museum und Allgemeine Zeitung*, February 23, 1837:

Deutsch

Deutsch zu seyn ist meine Freude,
Denn ich bin ein Deutscher doch;
Und die ächten deutschen Leute
Die sind mir am liebsten noch.

2

Deutsch will ich auch seyn und bleiben,
Weil ich deutsch geboren bin.
Deutsches Lesen, deutsches Schreiben,
Das, das geht nach meinem Sinn.

3

Deutsche Sitten und Manieren,
Deutsche Predigt und Gebet,
Das thut unser Deutschthum zieren,
Weil das Deutsch fein lieblich geht.

4

Deutsche Presse — deutsche Schulen,
Das macht unserm Deutschthum Ruhm.
Wer wollt' nicht um's Deutsche buhlen,
Als ein schönes Eigenthum?

5

Gieb mir deutschen Trank und Speise;
Gieb mir deutsche Kleidertracht:
Kurz, gieb mir die deutsche Weise,
Weil das Deutsch' mich freudig macht.

6

Laszt uns doch das Deutsche ehren,
Die wir noch ächt' Deutsche sind,
Dasz das Deutsch' sich möge mehren,
Und vom Vater geh'n zum Kind.

7

Mög' das Deutsch' doch recht aufkeimen,
In dem Nord-Amerika;
Möchten wir's auch nicht versäumen
Hier in Ober-Canada.

—J. B. (Probably Jacob Benner who, with Benjamin Eby and H. W. Peterson, was a trustee of the Berlin Public School for the year 1836. He was also a shareholder in Peterson's *Museum* to which he pledged twenty dollars.

Translation:

German

To be German is my pleasure,
For I'm German to the core;
Those who fill the German measure,
Are the ones whom I adore.

2

German I shall be forever,
Since a German I was born.
Reading, writing German ever,
Shall my heart and hand adorn.

3

German customs, German manners,
German prayer and sermon too,
Wave o'er German ways their banners,
Since in them they're ever new.

4

German press and German learning,
Hold aloft the German name.
Who can cease his German yearning,
Forever it exerts its claim?

5

German drink and fare I favor,
German dress is unsurpassed:
It's the German way I long for,
From the first until the last.

6

What is German, let us cherish,
We whose German blood runs true,
So that German here may flourish,
And from age to youth renew.

7
May then German seeds be growing,
In our North America;
Might its joys to us be flowing,
Here in Upper Canada.

5 Mrs. Anna Jameson, *Winter Studies and Summer Rambles in Canada*, (New York, 1839), I, p. 190.

6 W. H. Smith, *Canada: Past, Present and Future*, (Toronto, 1851), II, p. 118.

7 Bockstahler, O. L. "Schiller in Canada", *Modern Language Forum*. Vol. 25 (1940), pp. 125—132.

CHAPTER III

1 *Neu-Hamburger Neutrale*, January 19, 1855:

Prospectus

Die deutsche Bevölkerung in Canada hat sich in der jüngsten Zeit so ansehnlich gemehrt und der Drang nach Bildung ist unter unsern deutschen Landsleuten in einem so erfreulichen Maße gewachsen, daß die Herausgabe einer neuen deutschen Zeitschrift bei dem mit den Verhältnissen Vertrauten keiner Rechtfertigung bedarf.

Allerdings könnte es bei einer flüchtigen Betrachtung unserer örtlichen Verhältnisse auffällig erscheinen, daß in einem Orte, wie unser Neu-Hamburg ist, der den durch seinen Namen hervorgerufenen Ansprüchen auf Größe, Reichthum und Bildung erst in der Folgezeit genügen kann, zwei Wochenblätter erscheinen sollen, allein ein unbefangener Hinblick auf die Lage der Dinge wird diese auffällige Erscheinung genügend erklären. Es war sehr natürlich, daß jener obenerwähnte Wissensdrang unserer hier und in der Umgegend wohnenden Landsleute geistige Kräfte veranlassen mußte, demselben genügen zu wollen; allein leider scheint es den Männern, welche den Beruf in sich zu fühlen vermeinten, als Bildner und Lehrer des Volks aufzutreten, nicht gelungen zu sein, den Anforderungen, welche das lesende Publikum stellen durfte, in geeigneter Weise zu entsprechen.

Soll eine Zeitschrift in diesem Lande oder an diesem Orte von wirklichem Segen sein, so gilt es vor allen Dingen, den geistigen Zustand der Leser zu berücksichtigen. Dieses fordert aber—und wer möchte dies tadeln?—vor allem Achtung vor seinen religiösen Grundsätzen und Meinungen; ferner liegt ihm an einem Eingehen in seine eigenen Verhältnisse und einem Vermeiden aller widerwärtigen Privatstreitigkeiten; es verlangt schließlich eine Unterweisung in der fortlaufenden Weltgeschichte, und Mittheilungen aus dem reichen Felde der volksthümlichen Wissenschaft, die ihm zur Verschönerung des Lebens und zur Veredelung des Geistes dienen sollen. Dieß [sic] ist unsere Ansicht von der Art, wie eine Zeitschrift, die segensreich wirken will, in diesem Lande gehalten sein muß; und damit haben wir auch zugleich das Ziel angedeutet, welches wir uns bei der Herausgabe unseres *Neu-Hamburger Neutralen* vorgesteckt haben.

Unser Blatt stellt sich die Aufgabe, seinen Lesern ein treuer Führer in dem oft verworrenen Gange der Tagesgeschichte und auf dem reichen Felde der volksthümlichen Wissenschaft zu werden; es will ferner seine Freunde in ihrer neuen Heimat heimisch machen. Zur Erreichung dieses Zweckes werden wir über die Verhandlungen des Parlaments berichten und alle neuen Gesetze und Verordnungen in den Spalten unserer Zeitung bekannt machen. Um unsern Lesern die nöthige Kenntniß von den Tagesereignissen und von den Fortschritten in der Landeskultur zu verschaffen, haben wir uns mit den besten Hilfsmitteln versehen; auswärtige Freunde haben uns überdem ihre Mitwirkung zugesichert. Erzählungen endlich aus dem Volksleben, an denen sich Geist und Gemüth ergötzen, werden die noch übrigen Spalten unserer Zeitung füllen.

In diesem Sinne und mit diesen Vorsätzen wird der *Neu-Hamburger Neutrale* jeden Freitag regelmäßig erscheinen; und er wird mit derselben Ausdauer, welche ihn schier unübersteigliche Hindernisse bei seinem Hervortreten überwinden ließ, den einmal vorgezeichneten Lauf verfolgen. Wir hoffen schließlich, daß er auf demselben recht viele warme Freunde finden und gewinnen möge; es wird seine Sorge sein, sich dieselben zu erhalten.

Translation:

The German population in Canada has grown so considerably recently, and the urge for education has increased among our German compatriots in such gratifying measure, that the publication of a new German journal requires no justification among those familiar with the situation.

Naturally it might appear rather extraordinary on a superficial observation of our local conditions that in a village like our New Hamburg, which can only hope to satisfy at some future date the demands of magnitude, wealth and culture which its name suggests, two weeklies should appear; however, an unprejudiced view of the state of affairs will yield a sufficient explanation of this extraordinary phenomenon. It was very natural that the aforementioned urge for knowledge on the part of our compatriots living here and in the surrounding area, would call forth intellectual forces to satisfy the same; but unfortunately it seems that the individuals, who presumed to feel called upon to appear as molders and mentors of the people, did not succeed in coming up to the high expectations which the reading public would demand.

If a journal is to be a real blessing in this country or in this town, then it is absolutely necessary to take into account the intellectual state of the readers This demands—and who might take objection—respect particularly for their religious principles and opinions; further, there must be thorough familiarization with its peculiar circumstances and an avoidance of all vexatious private controversies and disputes; and finally it requires a pointing up of current world events and reports from the fertile field of popular science, which can serve for the embellishment of life and the ennobling of the spirit. This is our view of the manner in which a journal, which is to operate beneficially, must be conducted in this country; and thus we have also indicated the goal which we have set ourselves in the publication of our *New Hamburg Neutrale*.

Our paper has as its aim to become for its readers a true guide in the often confused course of daily events, and on the fertile field of popular science; it further wishes to make its friends feel at home in their new homeland. To achieve this goal we shall report the debates in parliament and publish all new laws and decrees in the columns of our newspaper. In order to provide our readers with the necessary information of the daily events and of the progress in the country's culture, we have provided ourselves with the best sources of material; friends abroad have in addition promised us their co-operation. Literary material from the life of the common people, to delight the mind and heart, will fill the remaining columns of our newspaper.
With this intention and with these principles the *New Hamburg Neutrale* will appear regulary every Friday, and will follow the prescribed path with the same perseverance with which it overcame the almost insurmountable obstacles to its appearance. We hope finally, that it may find and win a host of warm friends; it will make every effort to retain them.

2 *Neu-Hamburger Neutrale*, October 2, 1857:
Der Turnverein in Preston hat letzten Freitag sein jährliches Jubiläum gefeiert, wozu auch unsere Hamburger Turner höflichst eingeladen waren, welche am Sonntag Abends mit ihrem Banner wieder glücklich und ohne Rumor zurückgekehrt sind.
Der Erfolg des Turnens soll nicht geringhaltig gewesen sein, und das Lagerbier und—Brauhahn—sollen einen derben Schlag bekommen haben.
Uebrigens ist es sehr erfreulich und macht den Deutschen Ehre, daß ein solches Fest ohne Krawall geendet hat.

Translation:

The *Turnverein* (gymnastic club) in Preston celebrated its annual jubilee last Friday, to which our Hamburg *Turners* (gymnasts) were courteously invited. The latter returned again on Sunday evening safely with their banner and without any uproar.
The success of the gymnastic exercises is said to have been considerable, and the lager beer and—pale ale—are said to have taken a severe beating.

Nevertheless it is very gratifying and a credit to the Germans that such a festival ended without a row.

3 James Sutherland, *Counties of Perth and Waterloo Gazetteer and General Business Directory for 1870—71* (Ottawa and Toronto, 1869), p. 282.

4 *Canadian Newspaper Directory* (Toronto: Mail Newspaper Advertising Agency, 1884), p. 14.

5 Johannes Pietsch, *Bei den Deutschen in Westkanada* (Hünfeld, 1928), p. 79.

6 Karl Müller-Grote. *Onkel Karl. Deutsch-Kanadische Lebensbilder* (Bremen: Angelsachsen Verlag, 1924) pp. 44—45:

Dieses Mißverhältnis zwischen äußerer Aufmachung und innerm Gehalt trat auch bei . . . dem "Volksblatt" in die Erscheinung. An dem Format des immer noch von mir gelesenen "Reichsboten" . . . gemessen, war nicht nur das "Volksblatt", sondern auch alle anderen in den von Deutschen bewohnten Bezirken der Provinz Ontario erscheinenden Zeitungen ganz stattliche, durch saubern Druck sich auszeichnende Blätter; aber ein lesbarer Leitartikel war meist eine von außen hineingeschmuggelte Seltenheit, von der man nicht einmal behaupten konnte, daß sie einem sonderlich dringend empfundenen Bedürfnis der anspruchslosen Leser entsprochen hätte. Die waren durchaus befriedigt, wenn ihnen die Zeitung mitteilte, was die Verwandtschaft und die in näherer oder weiterer Umgebung wohnenden Landsleute trieben . . .

Da konnte man unter Karlsruhe, Heidelberg, Mannheim, Philippsburg usw. lesen: „Herr John Schweinsberger hat ein neues Dach auf seinen Hinkelstall gesetzt." „Hier wird jetzt mit dem Lattwerg-Kochen angefangen." „Die Frau von Peter Brubacher ist auf Besuch zu ihrer Tochter nach Straßburg gefahren" usw. Diese hochinteressanten Nachrichten über das Tun und Treiben der Abonnenten und deren Angehörigen füllten ganze Spalten der deutschen Wochenblätter. Und nun erst die Anzeigen! Bei ihrer Fassung hatten die Anpreisungen englischer Blätter als Vorbild gedient, und durch die oft wörtliche Übertragung des englischen Sprachgebrauchs entstand ein so verrücktes Deutsch, daß man nicht wußte, ob man sich darüber lustig machen oder sich ärgern sollte."

Translation:

This incongruity between external form and inner content also manifested itself . . . in the *Volksblatt*. When compared to the format of the *Reichsbote*, which I still continued to read, not only the *Volksblatt*, but all the other newspapers which appeared in the German-inhabited areas of the Province of Ontario were quite imposing, excellently printed journals, but a readable leading article was usually a rarity smuggled in from outside sources which could not be claimed to correspond to a particularly heartfelt need on the part of the unpretentious readers. These were satisfied completely when the paper informed them what their relatives and fellow countrymen at home or in distant parts were doing . . .

Thus one could read under the heading of Karlsruhe, Heidelberg, Mannheim, Philippsburg, etc., the following: „Mr. John Schweinsberger has put a new roof on his hen-house." „Here they are beginning to boil apple butter." „Mrs. Peter Brubacher is visiting her daughter in Strassburg" etc. These highly interesting items about the doings of the subscribers and their families filled whole columns of the German weeklies. But this was nothing compared to the advertisements. In their wording the extravagant language of English newspapers served as a model, and in the often literal rendition of the English original a German style was employed that was so crazy that one did not know whether to laugh or be annoyed at it.

7 *Canadisches Volksblatt*, October 21, 1891:

Patriotisch. — Am Dienstag voriger Woche also am Jahrestage der Schlacht von Queenston Heights wehte die Flagge auf dem Thurme unseres Schulhauses. Die Lehrer hielten Ansprachen an ihre Schüler und legten ihnen die historische Bedeutung des Tages aus. Das ist ein Schritt in der rechten Richtung und ist es sehr lobenswerth wenn Lehrer bemüht sind ihren Schülern Vaterlandsliebe einzuprägen.

Translation:
Patriotic. — On Tuesday of the past week, that is, on the anniversary of the battle of Queenston Heights, the flag waved on the bell tower of our schoolhouse. The teachers gave addresses and explained the historical significance of the day to their students. That is a step in the right direction and it is very praiseworthy when teachers make an effort to inculcate love of country in their students.

8 *Ibid.*, February 26, 1902:
... England war in der That das Land der wahren Freiheit in der Mitte des vorigen Jahrhunderts und wir müssen aufrichtig zugeben, es war gut, daß Albion damals an der Spitze der Civilisation marschirte. Bürgerliche Freiheit hat nirgends so schöne Blüthen gezeitigt als in dem meerumschlungenen Großbritannien. Darum lieben die deutschen Canadier die freien Institutionen Canadas und sind die loyalsten Subjekte seiner Majestät Königs Edwards VII. von England ...

Translation:
... England was indeed the land of true freedom in the middle of the past century. We must with all sincerity confess that it was good that Albion at that time marched in the forefront of civilization. Civic freedom nowhere matured such beautiful flowers as in our sea-girt Great Britain. For that reason the German Canadians venerate the free institutions of Canada and are the most loyal subjects of His Majesty Edward VII of England ...

9 *Ibid.*, December 5, 1906:

Germania

Das schönste Lied möcht ich dir weihen
Dir, Deutschthum in Amerika!
Dem edlen Stamm, dem großen, freien,
Den Kindern der Germania.
Dem alten Volk auf neuer Erde,
Das noch auf deutsche Sitte baut,
Und auch am neuen, heim'schen Herde
Verehrt der Muttersprache Laut.

Es war gar schwer, am fremden Orte
Zu pflegen deutschen Geist und Sinn,
Es ist gar schwer, dem deutschen Worte
Zu wahren Anseh'n und Gewinn.
Die Jugend hört mit and'ren Ohren,
Sie athmet eine and're Luft,
Und darum geht so leicht verloren
Der Muttersprache Blüthenduft.

Die alten Reihen sind gelichtet,
Die stolzen Eichen sterben aus,
Und was die Alten auch verrichtet,
Die Jugend macht sich nichts daraus.
O, schwer ist's, deutschen Sinn zu pflegen!
Wie oft sinkt mir der frohe Muth —
Ein and'rer Geist will sich hier regen
Man schätzt nicht mehr das theuere Gut!

Wohl gelten viele meiner Lieder
Der neuen Heimath, schön und frei!
Von oben thaue Segen nieder,
Daß sie der Freiheit Wohnsitz sei,

Das schönste aber will ich singen
Dem Deutschthum in Amerika,
Heut' soll es rauschen, soll es klingen:
Germania! Germania!

Translation:

Germania

I dedicate my sweetest song
To the Germans in America!
Who noble, free and great belong,
To the children of Germania.
To the old race on the new earth,
Which builds on German customs here,
And also on the new-found hearth,
The mother tongue still does revere.

No easy task in this strange land,
To foster German taste and mind;
Nor can the German word demand,
That proper place that it should find.
Our children foreign sounds now hear,
They breathe another, different air;
The mother tongue now rings less clear,
Its fragrance is no longer there.

The ranks once filled are sparse and thin,
The once proud oaks are felled and gone,
And what ancestral hands did win,
Our youth recks not what has been done.
From fostering German ways and mind,
My spirit quails and shrinks away,
To what once was we now are blind,
Its treasures hold no longer sway.

Full many a song that I have sung,
Extols this land, so fine and free.
May blessing down on it be flung,
May it the seat of freedom be.
Most sweetly shall I surely sing,
To the Germans in America,
Today let it resound and ring:
Germania! Germania!

10 *Ibid.*, May 20, 1908:

Deutsch

Die deutsche Sprache ist und bleibt
Die schönste Sprache doch,
Drum, Deutscher, halte jederzeit
In diesem Land sie hoch.

Verkenn, wenn du auch Englisch kannst,
Nicht ihren hohen Werth:
Es ist die Sprache, die dich einst
Die Mutter hat gelehrt.

In ihr stieg auf dein erst Gebet,
Und war's auch Lallen gleich,
Der liebe Gott verstand das Kind
In seinem Himmelreich.

Höhnt dich vielleicht der Nativist,
Vergib dem Mann die Schuld,

Er ist ein Narr, und diese soll
Man tragen mit Geduld.

Doch gänzliche Verachtung stets
Treff jeden deutschen Wicht,
Der seine schöne Muttersprach'
Nicht gern auch hier noch spricht.

Translation:

German

German is and shall be e'er,
The finest tongue, 'tis sure;
O Germans let it falter ne'er,
It must here, too, endure.

Its sterling worth do not reject,
Though English you might know;
It is the tongue you must respect,
Your mother taught you so.

In it did soar your childhood prayer,
Maybe in halting tone.
But our good Lord the child did hear,
Within his heavenly home.

The nativist's rude, scoffing voice,
Be not incensed thereby,
He is a fool, and will rejoice,
If it your patience try.

But lasting and complete disdain,
Strike every German wight,
Who does designedly refrain,
To speak his tongue aright.

11 Sutherland Bros., *County of Perth, Gazetteer and General Business Directory for 1863—64* (Ingersoll, C. W., 1863), p. 108.

12 *American Newspaper Directory* (New York: George P. Rowell and Co., Publishers, 1873), p. 232.

13 *Canadian Newspaper Directory* (Toronto: Mail Newspaper Advertising Agency, 1884), p. 12.

14 *American Newspaper Directory* (New York: George P. Rowell and Co., Publishers, 1873), p. 230.

15 *Pettengill's Newspaper Directory and Advertiser's Handbook for 1877* (New York: W. M. Pettengill and Co., 1877), p. 275.

16 *Der Deutsche Pionier* (Cincinnati: Herausgegeben vom „Deutschen Pionier-Verein", (1869—1887) VIII, p. 319.

17 *The County of Waterloo Gazetteer and Directory for 1877—78* (Toronto: Armstrong and Co., 1878), p. 104.

18 Heinrich Lemcke. *Canada, das Land und seine Leute* (Leipzig: Eduard Heinrich Mayer, 1887), p. 57.

19 *American Newspaper Directory* (New York: George P. Rowell and Co., Publishers, 1873), p. 233.

[20] *Canadian Newspaper Directory* (Toronto: Mail Newspaper Advertising Agency, 1884), p. 13.

[21] *Die Ontario Glocke*, December 13, 1893:
„Es werd doch allerweil fun nix als fun Prohibition geschwetzt. Mei Nochbor mehnt, wann die Mätschority dafor schtimmt, dann kriege mir sertenly Prohibition. 'Jo', hab ich gsagt, 'un die Kih fliege neckscht Frijohr uf die Weed, wann sie Fliegel kriege.' Ich hab keen Bang for de Temperenzleid; ich kenn sie zu gut. Sie mehne's net halb so schlimm wie sie kreische un riminder mich immer an den Buh den jemand gfrogt hot, ob sei Fader en Chrischt sei. 'Jo', hot er gsagt, 'awer er schafft net fiel dra!' Do neilich wor ich in ehre Temperenz-Meeting, der Leckstcherer hot gor jemmerlich iwer de Schnapps hergzoge un hot gmehnt: ‚Der Verbrauch fun berauschende Gedrenke in dem Land macht mich schwindlich.' Hinner in der Haal war en Mann, der sei beschtes browirt hot, um sich am Pleschter an der Wand in der Heh zu halde, der hot gekrische, 'mich ah!' "

[22] *Die Ontario Glocke*, March 20, 1889:
... Wir, als geborener Canadier, behaupten, daß die Deutschen und deren Kinder in Canada *in jeder Hinsicht* ebenso loyale Canadier sind, als die Eingewanderten aus Großbritannien und deren Nachkommen.
Auf was wir aber noch stolz und stets stolz sein werden ist, daß wir als Canadier auch die Sprache unserer Eltern verstehen und folglich eine Idee von deutschen Sitten, deutscher Literatur und dem herrlichen deutschen Liede haben. —

Translation:
... We, as a born Canadian, assert that the Germans and their children in Canada are *in every respect* as loyal Canadians as the immigrants from Great Britain and their descendants.
We are and will always be proud of the fact that we, as Canadians, also understand the language of our forefathers and consequently have an understanding of German customs, German literature and the magnificent German song. —

[23] *Deutsch-Amerikanisches Conversations-Lexicon*. Edited by Alexander J. Schem (New York, 1871), III, p. 18.

[24] *Ibid.*, XI (1873), p. 652.

[25] *American Newspaper Directory* (New York: George P. Rowell and Co., Publishers, 1873), p. 229.

[26] Wilhelm Joest, *Die außereuropäische deutsche Presse* (Köln, 1888), p. 83.

[27] *Berliner Journal*, June 11, 1874:
Dominion Tag. — Am 1. Juli Nachmittags wird im Stadtpark ein großes Picknick und abends in St. Nicholas Hall ein Ball der Handwerker, unter Mitwirkung des Musik-Chors, stattfinden. Wie aus der Anzeige zu ersehen, sind es wieder Deutsche, die Anstalten zur gemeinsamen Feier dieses Canadisch-nationalen Festtages treffen. Da sage noch so ein eingebildeter John Bull, die Deutschen von Berlin wären nicht loyal!
Translation:
Dominion Day. — On July first in the afternoon a big picnic will be held in the city park, and in the evening a mechanics' ball in St. Nicholas Hall with the co-operation of the music society. As one notices from the advertisement, it is again the Germans who are making the preparations for the public celebration of this national Canadian festival. Now let any conceited John Bull say that the Germans in Berlin are not loyal!

[28] *Berliner Journal*, June 24, 1875:
Dominion Tag. — Wenn die Deutschen in Berlin keine Anstalt treffen zur

Feier des Königingeburts- oder Dominion-Tages, dann geschieht auch nichts. So hat auch jetzt wieder unser strebsamer „Concordia"-Gesangverein in Verbindung mit dem städtischen Musik-Chor Schritte gethan zur Feier des 1. Juli. Nachmittags 1 Uhr werden Musiker und Sänger und alle Anderen, die sich an der Feier betheiligen, von der Stadthalle in Prozession nach dem Park ziehen, wo für Belustigungen verschiedener Art, sowie für Erfrischungen gesorgt wird. — Eine Platform zum Tanzen wird errichtet und des Abends der Hain mit Fackeln illuminirt, und das Comite wird sich bemühen, alles so einzurichten "gerade wie in Deutschland".

Translation:
Dominion Day. — If the Germans in Berlin make no preparations to celebrate the Queen's birthday or Dominion Day, then nothing at all is done. Again it is our methodical Concordia Society, in co-operation with the Philharmonic Choir, which has made the arrangements for the first of July celebration. At one o'clock in the afternoon the musicians and singers, and all others taking part in the celebration, will march in line from the City Hall to the park, where various types of entertainment and refreshments will be provided. — A platform for dancing will be constructed and in the evening the park will be illuminated with torches. The committee will make an effort to arrange everything "just as in Germany".

29 Clarence S. Brigham, *Journals and Journeymen* (Philadelphia: University of Pennsylvania Press, 1950), p. 84.

30 Gotthard Maron, "Die Deutschen in Canada", *Der Nordwesten-Kalender für das Jahr 1914* (Winnipeg: Der Nordwesten Publishing Company), p. 107.

CHAPTER IV

1 *Farmers and Business Directory for the Counties of Halton, Waterloo and Wellington* (Ingersoll: Union Publishing Company, XVI, 1906), opposite p. 268.

CHAPTER V

1 *Desbarats Newspaper Directory 1909—1910* (Montreal and Toronto: Desbarats Advertising Agency, 1910), p. 113.

2 *American Newspaper Annual and Directory* (Philadelphia: N. W. Ayer & Son, 1911), p. 1060.

3 *Canadian Almanac* (Toronto: Copp, Clark Company, 1911—1919).

4 W. S. Wallace, "The Periodical Literature of Upper Canada". *The Canadian Historical Review*, March 1931, pp. 4—5.

CHAPTER VI

1 *Canadisches Volksblatt*, February 26, 1896:
Es giebt viele Deutsche welche glauben, daß Alles was sie in englischen Zeitungen lesen, gut und neu, Alles, was sie in deutschen lesen, schlecht und veraltet sei. Es fehlt denen eben zur richtigen Beurtheilung das nöthige Wissen. Rascher urtheilt die englische Presse allerdings: sie ist daher auch voller Vorurtheile, die deutsche Presse hingegen gewissenhafter und gründlicher, in Folge dessen allerdings auch langsamer; sie wird dadurch aber für den Leser ein zuverlässiger Rathgeber.

Translation:
There are many Germans who believe that everything that they read in the English newspapers is accurate and new; everything that they read in the German newspapers inaccurate and out of date. These readers simply lack the knowledge necessary to make a valid judgment. To be sure, the English press gives an opinion more quickly: it is therefore also more prejudiced; the German press, on the other hand, more conscientious and more thorough,

in consequence, to be sure, somewhat slower, but because of that a reliable guide for the reader.

[2] Heinz Lehmann, "Deutsche Zeitung für Canada", *Deutsche Arbeit* XXXV (September, 1935), p. 484.

[3] *Deutsch-Amerikanisches Conversations-Lexicon*. Edited by Alexander J. Schem (New York), III (1871), p. 18.

[4] Heinz Lehmann. *Zur Geschichte des Deutschtums in Kanada. Band I, Das Deutschtum in Ostkanada* (Stuttgart, 1931), p. 114.

[5] Ernst Feise, "Colonial Petrification", *German Quarterly* XIII (May, 1940), pp. 117—124.

[6] Albert Bernhardt Faust. *The German Element in the United States* (New York, 1927), II, pp. 365—66.

[7] *Berliner Journal*, November 29, 1894:

CANADA
Melodie: "Die Wacht am Rhein"

I

Du Canada, du schönes Land,
Du bist mein theures Vaterland.
Dir bleib ich ewig gut und treu,
Ob Wohnort auch im Fremdland sei!

Lieb Canada, du schönes Land
Lieb Canada, du freies Land,
Du bist und bleibst mein liebes Vaterland,
Du bist und bleibst mein theures Vaterland.

II

Du glücklich' großes Canada
Bist reich fürwahr, Halleluja! —
Hast Gold und Silber, Eisen, Erz —
Korn, Weizen, Gerste allerwärts. —

Lieb Canada, du schönes Land, etc.

III

Auch ruf' ich's laut wie Donnerhall,
Gesetze hast — nicht groß an Zahl! —
Die besten aber in der Welt
Hast du dein'm Volke hingestellt! —

Lieb Canada, du schönes Land, etc.

IV

Ein Vivat-Hoch, dir liebes Land —
Du bist und bleibst mein Vaterland.
Ob's herrlich in der Fremd' auch sei,
Dir bleib ich ewig fest und treu!

Lieb Canada, du schönes Land, etc.

EXTANT
ONTARIO GERMAN NEWSPAPERS
1835—1918

The following files, broken files, and individual copies of Ontario German newspapers were employed in the preparation of this history:

Place of Publication	*Publication*
Berlin	*Canada Museum und Allgemeine Zeitung* (Volume 1, number 1, August 27, 1835, to volume 5, number 26, December 18, 1840)
Waterloo	*Der Morgenstern* (Volume 1, numbers 34, March 12, 1840; 41, May 7, 1840; 46, June 25, 1840. Volume 2, August 27, 1840 to September 16, 1841.)
Berlin	*Der Deutsche Canadier und Neuigkeitsbote* (Volume 1, number 35, August 27, 1841. Volume 4, 1844. Volume 5, 1845. Volume 8, 1848 to volume 20, 1860. Volume 27, number 44, November 12, 1867.)
Preston New Hamburg	*Der Canadische Beobachter* (Volume 2, number 6, February 8, 1849. Volume 7, number 5, February 9, 1855 to volume 8, number 6, February 15, 1856.)
New Hamburg	*Neu-Hamburger Neutrale* (Volume 1, number 1, Januar 19, 1855 to December 28, 1855. Volume 3, number 1, January 2, 1857 to December 25, 1857.)
Preston Waterloo	*Der Canadische Bauernfreund* (Volume 2, number 17, February 27, 1852. Volume 3, number 21, March 25, 1853. Volume 18, number 29, May 14, 1868.)
Berlin Kitchener	*Berliner Journal* (Volume 1, number 1, December 29, 1859 to volume 58, number 2, January, 1917; *Ontario Journal*, January 10, 1917 to October 2, 1918 (One year, 1910, is missing from the files.)
New Hamburg	* *Canadisches Volksblatt* (Volume 5, number 19, May 12, 1859. Volume 11 to volume 18, January 5, 1865 to December 18, 1872. Volume 22, number 15, April 12, 1876. Volume 25, 1879 in which numbers 1 to 5, 29 and 51 are missing. Volume 28, 1882 in which numbers 14, 29, 42 and 44 to the end of the year are missing. Volume 30, 1884 with extant numbers 3—5, 12—19, 21, 24—30, 36—41, 49 and 50. Volume 35, number 9, February 29, 1888. Volume 36, 1889, with extant numbers 1, 6, 10, 21, 26 and from number 39, October 2, 1889, to volume 56, number 49, December 2, 1908.)
Waterloo	*Der deutsche Reformer* (Volume 1, number 1, June 6, 1863.)
Stratford	*Der Canadische Kolonist* (Volume 9, number 48, December 4, 1872. Volume 21, number 50, December 17, 1884.)
Elmira	*Elmira Anzeiger* (Volume 4, number 13, April 17, 1873. Volume 6, number 22, June 17, 1875. Volume 7, number 29, August 3, 1876. Volume 10, number 21, June 5, 1879. Volume 11, number 8, March 4, and number 36, September 16, 1880.)
Walkerton	*Die Ontario Glocke* (Volume 14, number 1, January 3, 1883 to volume 29, number 52, December 28, 1898.)

Berlin	*Berlin Daily News* (German section) (Volume 1, number 1, February 9, 1878 to October 16, 1878.)
Stratford	*Der Perth Volksfreund* (Volume 1, number 21, November 29, 1878.)
Berlin	*Das Wochenblatt* (Volume 1, number 2, February 26, and number 3, March 5, 1878.)
Berlin	*Freie Presse* (Volume 1, number 1, August 6, 1886, to August 5, 1887.)
Berlin	*Deutsche Zeitung* (Volume 1, number 1, November 3, 1891 to volume 8, number 52, October 11, 1899.)

* Mr. Ernst Ritz, New Hamburg, Ontario, has all the extant files of the *Canadisches Volksblatt* except volumes 11 and 12.

All others, with the exception of volumes 2 and 3 of the *Canada Museum und Allgemeine Zeitung*, are in the collections of the Waterloo Historical Society, Kitchener Public Library, Kitchener, Ontario.

BIBLIOGRAPHY

American Newspaper Annual and Directory. Philadelphia: N. W. Ayer and Son, 1911.

American Newspaper Directory. New York: Geo. P. Rowell & Co., 1873.

Bockstahler, O. L. "Schiller in Canada", *Modern Language Forum.* Vol. 25 (1940).

Brigham, Clarence S. *Journals and Journeymen.* Philadelphia: University of Pennsylvania Press, 1950.

Byerly, A. E. *The Beginning of Things in Wellington and Waterloo Counties.* Guelph: Guelph Publishing Company, 1935.

Canada: An Encyclopedia. Edited by J. Castell Hopkins. Article "A Review of Canadian Journalism". (Toronto, 1899).

Canada Directory for 1857—58. Montreal: John Lovell, 1857.

Canadian Almanac. Toronto: Copp, Clark Company, 1911—1919.

Canadian Dominion Directory for 1871. Montreal: John Lovell, 1871.

Canadian Newspaper Directory. 6th ed. Montreal and Toronto: A. McKim, Limited, 1909.

Canadian Newspaper Directory. Toronto: Mail Newspaper Advertising Agency, 1884.

County of Perth Gazetteer and General Business Directory for 1863—4. Ingersoll, C. W.: Sutherland Bro's., 1863.

Counties of Perth and Waterloo Gazetteer and General Business Directory for 1870—71. Compiled by James Sutherland, Ottawa and Toronto: Hunter, Rose & Co., 1869.

County of Waterloo Gazetteer and Directory for 1877—78. Toronto: Armstrong and Co., 1878.

Desbarats Newspaper Directory, 1909—1910. Montreal and Toronto: Desbarats Advertising Agency, 1910.

Deutsch-Amerikanisches Conversations-Lexicon. Edited by Alexander J. Schem. New York: E. Steiger, 1869—1874.

Deutsche Pionier, Der. Erinnerungen aus dem Pionier-Leben der Deutschen in Amerika. Cincinnati, Ohio: Herausgegeben vom "Deutschen Pionier Verein", 1869—1887.

Directory of the Province of Ontario for 1882. Montreal: John Lovell, 1882.

Farmers and Business Directory for the Counties of Halton, Waterloo and Wellington. Ingersoll: Union Publishing Company, 1906.

Faust, Albert Bernhardt. *The German Element in the United States.* Vol. II, *Journalism.* New York: The Steuben Society of America, 1927.

Feise, Ernst. "Colonial Petrification", *German Quarterly,* XIII (May, 1940).

Forty-Eigthers, The. Edited by A. E. Zucker. New York: Columbia University Press, 1950.

Friedmann, Wolfgang G. *German Immigration into Canada.* Contemporary Affairs — No. 23. Toronto: The Ryerson Press, 1952.

Hofacker, Erich P. "German Literature as Reflected in the German Language Press of St. Louis Prior to 1898", *Washington University Studies—New Series, Language and Literature*—No. 16 (Saint Louis, 1946).

Jameson, Mrs. Anna. *Winter Studies and Summer Rambles in Canada.* New York: Wiley and Putnam, 1839.

Joest, Wilhelm. *Die außereuropäische deutsche Presse*. Köln, 1888.

Kloss, Heinz. *Ahornblätter. Deutsche Dichtung aus Kanada*. Würzburg: Holzner-Verlag, 1961.

Kloss, Heinz. *"Materialien zur Geschichte der Deutschkanadischen Presse,"* Vol. XI. *Der Auslanddeutsche* (Stuttgart, 1928).

Lehmann, Heinz. *Das Deutschtum in Westkanada*. Berlin: Junker und Dünnhaupt, 1939.

Lehmann, Heinz. "Deutsche Zeitung für Canada", "Zur Geschichte der deutschkanadischen Presse", *Deutsche Arbeit*, XXXV (September, 1935).

Lehmann, Heinz. *Zur Geschichte des Deutschtums in Kanada. Band I. Das Deutschtum in Ostkanada*. Stuttgart: Ausland und Heimat Verlags-Aktiengesellschaft, 1931.

Lemcke, Heinrich. *Canada, das Land und seine Leute*. Leipzig: Eduard Heinrich Mayer, 1887.

Maron, Gotthard. "Die Deutschen in Canada". *Der Nordwesten-Kalender für das Jahr 1914*, Winnipeg: Der Nordwesten Publishing Company, 1914.

Middleton, Jesse Edgar and Landon, Fred (eds.). *The Province of Ontario—A History*. Toronto, 1927.

Mitchell's Canada Gazetteer and Business Directory for 1864—65. Toronto: W. C. Chewett and Co., 1864.

Mott, Frank Luther. *American Journalism*. New York: Macmillan, 1945.

Müller-Grote, Karl. *Onkel Karl. Deutsch-kanadische Lebensbilder*. Bremen: Angelsachsen Verlag, 1924.

Needler, G. H. *Colonel Anthony van Egmond*. Toronto: Burns and MacEachern, 1956.

Newspaper Directory and Advertiser's Handbook for 1877. New York: S. M. Pettengill and Co., 1877.

Oppel, Alwin. "Das Deutschtum in Kanada", *Deutsche Erde*, IV (Gotha, 1905).

Pietsch, Johannes. *Bei den Deutschen in Westkanada*. Hünfeld, 1928.

Pocket Directory of the American Press for 1916. Chicago: Lord and Thomas, 1916.

Smith, W. H. *Canada: Past, Present and Future*. Vol. II. Toronto: Thomas Maclear, 1851.

Stewart, J. J. "Early Journalism in Nova Scotia", *Collections of the Nova Scotia Historical Society, 1887—88*. Vol. VI (Halifax, 1888).

Taubert, Sigfred. "Die frühesten deutschen Drucker in Canada", *Börsenblatt für den Deutschen Buchhandel*—Frankfurter Ausgabe—Nr. 38 a, 14. Mai 1956.

Thomas, Isaiah. *The History of Printing in America*. Albany, N. Y.: Joel Munsell, 1874.

Uttley, W. V. (Ben). *A History of Kitchener, Ontario*. Kitchener, 1937.

Wallace, W. S. "The Periodical Literature of Upper Canada", *Canadian Historical Review*, XII (March, 1931).

Waterloo Historical Society, Annual Reports. Berlin, Kitchener: Published by the Society, 1913—1951.

Wittke, Carl. *The German-Language Press in America*. University of Kentucky Press, 1957.

INDEX OF NAMES

Lightning Source UK Ltd.
Milton Keynes UK
UKHW010012210722
406167UK00002B/482

9 780802 015792